Rubber Powered Model Airplanes

Don Ross
Comprehensive Building And
Flying Basics Plus Advanced
Design-Your-Own Instruction

An AViation Publishers Book
Published by *Markowski International Publishers*
Hummelstown, PA USA

Published by:
AViation Publishers
Markowski International Publishers
One Oakglade Circle, Hummelstown, PA 17036 USA
(717) 566-0468

Library of Congress Cataloging in Publication Data

Ross, Don
Rubber Powered Model Airplanes.
1. Airplanes–Models–Rubber Motors. I.Title
TL770.R667 1988 629.133'134 88-13066
ISBN 0-938716-19-0 (pbk.)

On The Cover

The lovely Beautiful Bess biplane designed by Charles Wood in 1953, built by Don Ross and flown by John Wilde. Cover transparency by Sid Bernstein.

Publisher's Note

Markowski International books are also available at discounts in bulk quantity for industrial or sales-promotional use. For details, contact Special Sales Manager at the Publisher's phone above.

DEDICATION

To my wife, Doris and daughters Julie and Marjorie who were always there, for Matthew Evan and computer wizard Gary Ross.

ACKNOWLEDGEMENT

This book could not have been written and published without the help and encouragement of a great many fine people. It seems quite unfair to merely list them when their contributions deserve so much more. Their ideas add immeasurably to the reader's knowledge: David Aronstein, Rich Fiore, Paul Kaufmann, Ken Naylyn, Walt Balcer, Mike Gretz, Larry Kruse, Leo McCarthy, Bob Bender, Bill Hartwell, Mike Liebman, Dick Nelson, Sid Bernstein, Bob Hatschek, Bob Lipori, Henry Nelson, Mark Fineman, Bob Hunt, Mike Markowski, Leo McCarthy, William F. McCombs, Jim O'Reilly, Frank Finelli, Bob Meuser, Tony Peters, Bob and Sandy Peck, Fernando Ramos, Art Reiners, Gene Scheppers, Walt Schwarz, George Schroeder, Al Smith, Marty Taft, Don Typond, Gary Inderwood, Joe Wagner, Barnaby Wainfan, Ed Whitten, John Wilde and Ron Williams. Special thanks also go to Jim Kaman for his fine illustrations throughout the book. They simplify and enhance the text wherever they appear.

Contents

Introduction

"Silent Magic" is a fair description of rubber powered model airplane flight. With their delicate structures etched against the sky like floating thoughts these craft have captured the imaginations of young and old long before Kitty Hawk. Now that the Voyager and the Gossamer Condor have rekindled interest in low, slow flight a whole new generation needs to walk the same path as Lindbergh, Grissom, MacCready, Yeager and Sally Ride.

This book is designed to take the new modeler through a series of practical, non-technical steps from a simple first model to a contest or sport level airplane capable of stable, sustained flight.

For the experienced modeler it contains a considerable storehouse of techniques, hints and plans drawn from 40 years of building and designing. New methods and materials added to basic procedures for building and flight trimming will enhance the skills at any level and provide better understanding of free flight aerodynamics.

For the parent intending to help the young builder, emphasis is on the "How-To" not the "Where-From" with a program of kits, tools and methods illustrated in clear stages that lead to good flights from the first model.

For the contest minded, a careful study of the chapters on finishing, weight saving, winding and trimming should turn a novice into a better than average competitor.

1

Canarsie Canary

The day I reported for my first real flying lesson I expected to spend hours being familiarized with the airplane and all the controls and instruments. Instead, with the plane already pre-flighted, my instructor installed me in the left seat, climbed aboard and said, "Let's go flying." We took off from Teterboro and as soon as we left the pattern I was given control and told to "Keep her straight and level."

I found out later that this abrupt introduction to flight is fairly standard. It gives the new student confidence and incentive to get airborne by himself as soon as he can.

I think modeling can be handled the same way. The Canarsie Canary was designed by Marty Taft (who is, of course, from Brooklyn) as a first model yet it is capable of 30 seconds or more of indoor flight and, with larger rubber, one minute outdoors. This may not sound like much but at a climb rate of 400 feet a minute this little design has been known to go "out of sight" (OOS) with only a little thermal help.

SO . . ., Let's Go Flyin'.

The tools required to build the Canary are simple and available in most homes or the nearest hardware store: single edged razor or hobby knife, scissors, nose pliers, pins, steel straight edge or scale, good modeler's glue (see glue chapter), and a square or right triangle.

One sheet of medium 1/32" x 2" balsa, one balsa stick 1/8" x 3/8" x 15", a Sig 5½" prop with hanger, 24" of 1/8" rubber, some tissue, stiff paper, a pin and a rubber band are all the materials you need to enter the world of free flight rubber modeling.

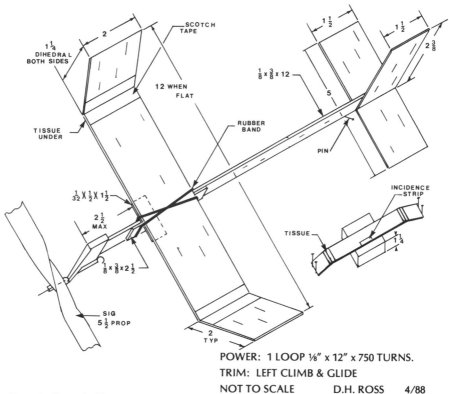

POWER: 1 LOOP ⅛″ x 12″ x 750 TURNS.
TRIM: LEFT CLIMB & GLIDE
NOT TO SCALE   D.H. ROSS   4/88

Fig. 1-1. Canarsie Canary.

Note that Fig. 1-1 shows small dashed or wiggly lines on the wood parts. These indicate the direction of the grain to guide you in cutting for maximum strength and minimum warp.

Fig. 1-2 shows the Sig Cub with all parts labeled. This will be a good reference for all plans and descriptions.

First cut the motor stick (1/8″ x 3/8″) to 12″ long. Then cut another piece 2½″ long for the wing platform. Then from the 1/32″ sheet cut first the 12″ x 2″ wing then the 5″ x 1½″ stab and the 2⅜″ x 1½″ rudder. Note that the wing and stab grains run parallel to their span but the rudder grain is vertical. This puts the strength where we need it most.

Lay the wing down flat and *lightly* make two small marks at the 6″ center and 2″ from each end. Lay a piece of scotch tape from front to rear centered over the "Tick" marks at the 2″ points. Now turn the wing over and score by lightly stroking with a razor or the back of a hobby knife at the 2″ points so the wing will crack here. *DO NOT* cut through and *DO NOT* score at the center mark.

Cut a 1½″ piece from the 1/32″ x 1/2″ scrap you saved and glue it to the center of the *leading edge (LE)* of the bottom of the wing. This is called the

6

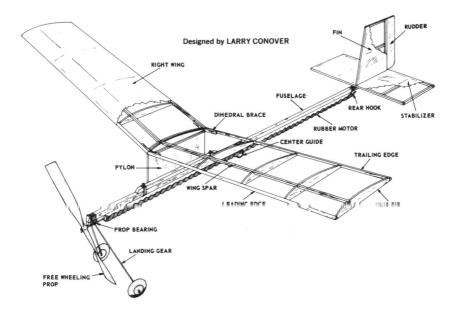

Designed by LARRY CONOVER

RIGHT WING

FIN

RUDDER

FUSELAGE

REAR HOOK

DIHEDRAL BRACE

STABILIZER

RUBBER MOTOR

CENTER GUIDE

TRAILING EDGE

PYLON

WING SPAR

LEADING EDGE

WING RIB

PROP BEARING

LANDING GEAR

FREE WHEELING
PROP

FIG. 1-2. Sig Cub showing parts of model.

"Incidence Strip" and is essential to the stability of the Canary.

Turn the wing over so the incidence strip is on the bottom and holding a straight edge along the score line (you will see the tick marks through the scotch tape), crack the wing upward. This is the most important part of the assembly and should be handled with care. The "Dihedral" you are creating by tilting the wing tips up at an angle will keep your model from crashing to one side or the other during a turn.

Gluing the wing at the proper angle can be done by laying the wing *UPSIDE DOWN* over a small block (a book or pet food can will do) and taping or pinning it to your board. Make sure both angles are the same then run a bead of glue along the crack and work it into the wood. See the sketch on the plan. This is the most important joint on the plane and will get the most punishment so a bit of care and patience will really pay off. A more accurate way to build dihedral is to block up both wing tips at the same time as shown in Fig. 1-3.

Allow one hour for the glue to dry thoroughly. Most glues dry from the outside in and many a modeler has been badly fooled by the "dry" feel of the outside of a glue joint while the inside where the strength is most needed is still in a putty like condition.

After the dihedral joint is fully dry, cut two small pieces of tissue about ½" x 2" and glue them over the joints on the bottom of the wing which is

7

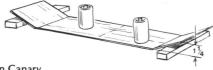

FIG. 1-3. Dihedral on Canary.

the side opposite the scotch tape.

During the time the wing is drying, assemble the rest of the model. Glue the stab to the bottom rear of the motor stick as shown. Glue the rudder assembly (the 1½″ x 2⅜″ piece) to the right side of the motor stick on top of the stab. (Fig. 1-4)

Cut two pieces of stiff bond paper (3″ x 5″ card, typewriter paper or stationery will do) ½″ x 1″ and attach them to the rudder and left wing as shown.

Note that right and left on a model are always designated as if you were in the pilot's seat.

A couple of pieces of scotch tape over the wing leading and trailing

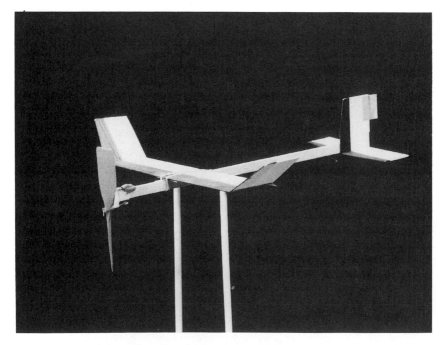

FIG. 1-4. Canary balanced on dowels.

edges will help prevent wear and cracking from the wing mounting rubber band.

Now the model can be decorated with magic marker and your name and address added somewhere prominent.

The wing is assembled to the motor stick using a medium rubber band and the wing saddle piece to prevent rocking. Push a heavy straight pin into the bottom of the motor stick as shown and add the prop hanger and prop to the front.

To make your model climb higher, eliminate the wing saddle, cut a strip ⅛" x ⅜" x 3" and glue it to the bottom center of the wing after attaching the incidence strip. Bind this "Pylon" (see Fig. 1-2) to the top of the motor stick with rubber bands.

Flying The Canary

Before attempting any flights, balance the model by sliding the wing forward or back until it sits level with a finger tip under the center of each wing. If the leading edge of the wing must be moved more than 2½" from the nose then add a bit of clay to the nose. Everyone hates to add any weight to a model but proper balance is much more important than a small weight gain. Remember, a free flight model must adjust itself in flight with no pilot at the controls. Fig. 1-4 shows my Canary in a balancing fixture.

Now skip to the chapter on flight trim and follow the Canary section to get your model into the air. As you fly the Canary, keep testing the plastic prop bearing for wobble. These will sometimes wear the nose of a soft motor stick very quickly and allow the rubber tension to bend the bearing down so the prop is at an angle and the model stops climbing. A hard wood splinter or toothpick glued into the nose, as in Fig. 1-5, will cure this.

I hope this chapter will get you started in modeling as painlessly and successfully as possible while teaching you some of the terminology and building techniques used on more complicated models.

The Canary is extremely rugged and will last through a lot of experiments. Make notes of each flight and when you finally "re-kit" the Canary in a fatal crash, build another.

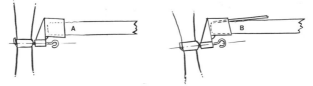

FIG. 1-5. Toothpick filler for loose prop hanger.

2

Wood Selection

Professionals say that the three most important things in real estate are location, location and location. The same thing might be said of weight in model airplanes. Certainly, good design and careful construction are important and so is appearance in scale models. However, this book is about "Flying" models and it is the weight the wing must carry that most often dictates how high the model will climb and, therefore, how easily it will find lifting air for those long flights. Also, since impact is mass times velocity, a heavy model has two strikes against it since it must fly faster for the wing to lift its mass and its own weight will increase any crash damage.

Good design will help save weight and many of the construction techniques in the next chapter will save even more with no loss in strength. Good wood selection, however, can do the most to give you a light, strong model that builds and repairs easily.

Before you begin to worry about becoming an expert in lumber psychology, history and economics let me point out that you will have only 3 factors to consider and one of them is printed on the wood. That doesn't sound so hard, does it?

The first factor to consider is the density of the wood. This is simply the weight in pounds of one cubic foot of balsa. Four to six pound wood is the lightest and should be used in areas where support strength and impact resistance are less important. Tail structures, nose area fill-in, fuselage planking, rear fuselage uprights, wing or tail cap strips and wing or tail leading edge planking are good areas for light balsa. Eight to ten pound

Table 2-1. Balsa density chart.

Sheet Thickness	1/32					1/16					3/32				1/8			
Density lbs/cu ft Size	4	5	6	8	10	4	5	6	8	10	4	6	8	10	4	6	8	10
2 x 36	2.4	3.0	3.6	4.8	6.0	4.7	5.8	7.1	9.3	11.7	7.0	10.5	14	17.5	9.4	14.1	18.9	23.6
3 x 36	3.6	4.5	5.4	7.2	9.0	7.1	8.7	10.5	14.0	17.5	10.5	15.9	21	26.3	14.1	21.2	28.3	35.4
4 x 36	4.3	6.0	7.2	9.7	12.1	9.4	11.7	14.1	18.7	23.4	14.1	21	28.1	35.1	18.9	28.4	37.7	47.1

GRAMS PER SHEET

balsa is the most common and will make good ribs, fuselage longerons, wing tips and nose blocks.

Desired density can be ordered from Sig, FAI or Champion and will be marked on the sheet or bundle. Ten to twelve pound balsa is hard to cut, carve and sand and has only a few special applications.

Table 2-1 shows how to convert the weight of a specific sheet into density. Table 2-2 shows suggested applications.

Table 2-2. Gram And Density Use Recommendations.

4-6 LB. A GRAIN: RIBS, SHEET TAILS, NOSE FILL-IN, PLANKING, CAP STRIPS
7-8 LB. A GRAIN: UPRIGHTS, FORMERS, PROPS, NOSE BLOCKS, T.E.
7-8 LB. C GRAIN: LONGERONS, L.E., SPARS, STRINGERS, FORMED TIPS

The next factors are hardness and "springiness." These are important and a little care here will allow the builder to put strength (and extra weight) only where needed. The appearance of the surface of the wood will help in determining the grain direction which is an indication of hardness. If the balsa shows long clear grain lines it is called "A" grain and is also usually very light, almost white in color. This is the most flexible type *across* the grain (the short dimension of the sheet — 3″ or 4″) and can be used for sheet covering of curved surfaces and light, flexible spars. Do not use for sheet balsa wings, tails or fuselage sides.

Balsa that shows a mottled or "Marbled" appearance is "C" grain and is very stiff across the sheet and splits easily but is the most warp resistant. This is sometimes called "Quarter Grain." "C" grain is best for sheet wings, tail and fuselages, wing ribs and formers. Do not use "C" grain for curved planking or carved nose blocks and propellers.

The springiness of a sheet or strip is best judged by a hand test (Fig. 2-1). Simply place the sheet or strip on a table edge with most of it

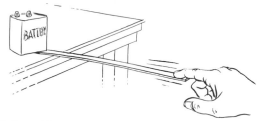

FIG. 2-1. Spring test on strips.

extended. Bend the strip down a few inches and observe the spring-back. In four tries you will be an expert. This test will help you choose the correct wood for each job. Fuselage longerons and wing leading edges should be the hardest, springiest wood you have.

The last test for balsa is the simplest. Just dig your fingernail into the sheet. Some will resist almost as much as hard wood. These will be "C" grain and with this test you can segregate the hardest sheets.

You may have noticed that "B" grain seems to be missing. "B" is something of a combination of "A" and "C". It shows long grain but is

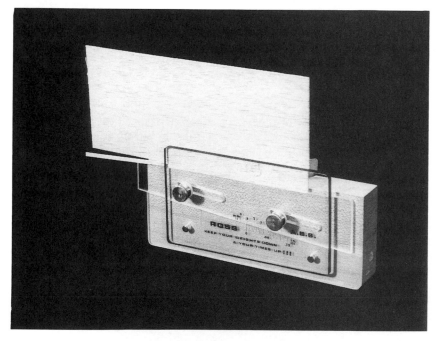

FIG. 2-2. Jim Jones balsa stripper.

12

also mottled. When I find sheets like that I usually apply the spring and hardness test and put the sheet into "A" or "C" bin depending on whether it shows soft (A) or hard (C).

With a balsa stripper you can be sure all the strips cut from one sheet will have the same properties thus helping to eliminate warps and twists due to unequal stiffness. Fig. 2-2 shows a good one made by Jim Jones.

If the builder will read the above just twice and spend ten minutes experimenting with a few sheets he will save many hours of repair time and will have models that will fly better.

The next chapter will show how some hardwoods like Bass and Bamboo can add great strength without extra weight.

3

Construction

I noticed during the beginner's classes I've taught that some of the basic skills in construction seem to have been lost. We have been working with "Snap-Together" plastic models and foam "Almost-Ready-to-Fly" (ARF) models for so long that even the fathers of my students have never seen a stick and tissue rubber model. Therefore, let's start with the real basics of cutting, gluing and sanding.

When cutting with a hobby knife or single edged razor, it is important to try to hold the blade as square as possible to the wood so the edge of the cut piece provides a close fit for gluing. Wherever possible use a straight edge or template to cut against. Draw the blade smoothly towards you along the cut. Don't try to cut through on one pass. Several shallow cuts are a lot better. Fig. 3-1 illustrates this.

Buy a package of 100 Exacto type blades for $5 or $6 and change frequently. I use about three blades for a 24" wingspan model. When cutting across the grain to the edge of the sheet, make a small notch at the edge you are cutting towards then proceed with several passes. This will keep the sheet from splitting as you approach the edge. Also, try to lay out your sheet parts so the grain is parallel with the longest dimension unless you need the strength the other way. For instance, a sheet of 3" x 36" will resist cracking best when the bend line is perpendicular to the 36" dimension. When cutting sheet parts (ribs and formers), always cut to compress the grain and resist splits.

Since the strength of a glue joint is almost directly proportional to its area, a good, square end on the sticks you cut is important. It will not only insure better alignment, your model will resist impacts much longer. Most people have trouble holding a blade exactly square. That's why I developed the little "Chopper" tool (Fig. 3-2). Just place a stick in proper

FIG. 3-1. Cut at 90 degrees.

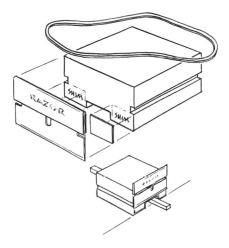

FIG. 3-2. Portable chopper for square cuts.

position on the plan then put the slot in the bottom of the chopper over the stick with the razor edge right on the cutting line. The pressure of the razor on the stick will hold it while you press down for a perfect cut.

When splices are needed to create longer sticks or to join two sticks at an angle, cut the sticks one over the other and at a long angle before joining so there is as much glue area as practical. Fig 3-3 shows two methods. Please try not to use sticks that come out a bit short. Either save them for another place or throw them out. If you are using a balsa stripper the cost is negligible. You see, glue generally shrinks as it dries. Therefore, when you try to fill a gap with glue it will pull on the surrounding wood and create warps and weak joints. A stick or sheet part should be a snug fit in place, just tight enough so it will hold without pins

15

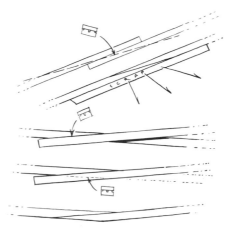

FIG. 3-3. Two splice methods.

but not forced in. If the stick is a bit too big then touch it up with a sanding block. Don't try to shave it with a blade.

I have found that by pinning down my longerons or wing leading and trailing edges, then cutting all ribs or uprights and trial fitting before gluing, I get a better structure and build faster.

Gluing: White Glue

Proper gluing technique will save weight, add strength and improve the appearance of any model. There are four basic types of glue and each requires different handling. Let's start with "White" glue which is the safest and one of the easiest to use. The best of the "White" type glues is usually called "Carpenter's Glue" and is an Aliphatic type. Many brands are available in your local hardware store. One of the good ones is "Wilhold." Elmers is not an Aliphatic and is not as strong. Most white glues are soluble in water, non-toxic and solvent proof when dry so doping will not affect them. "Sig-Bond" and "Quicksand" are designed for modeling. They dry quickly and sand easily.

I have found that a mixture of two parts glue to one part water works well. You can easily get a small Polyethylene squeeze bottle in the local drugstore. Some come with a small, screw-on nozzle that is perfect for dispensing glue. With this you can pre-mix your glue and store it in small quantities. For gluing sticks, Jesse Aronstein has a useful hint. He drops a small puddle of thinned glue on a piece of plastic. Then he simply dips the end of each stick in it, wipes off any excess and assembles. The thinned glue will penetrate the wood grain making a very strong joint with only one application (Fig. 3-4).

16

FIG. 3-4. Puddle of white glue in plastic container top.

Clean-up with water is easy but be careful of warps when "ungluing" a joint with water. White glue should be used whenever joining hard wood (bass, pine, spruce or plywood) to balsa. Also, white glue can be used to adhere tissue to balsa. This is discussed in the "Covering" chapter. White glue is not very good for attaching metal parts such as landing gear to wood. Use epoxy for this.

Gluing: Acetone Glue

"Glue Sniffing" has certainly tarnished the reputation of the solvent of Acetone glues, yet many millions use them with proper care and have no trouble. Follow the directions on the tube, work with good ventilation and close the tube when not in use. I don't usually thin my Acetone glues but I "Double Glue" most joints.

Just apply a very small amount of glue to both sides of the joint. Wipe off any excess and allow ten minutes to dry. Then apply another small amount to only one side and assemble. You will find this actually speeds up your assembly work.

This allows the first application to penetrate the grain and seal the surface. I find this not only makes a stronger joint, the glue dries almost as fast as one of the "Instant" types.

Acetone glue is more flexible than white glue so it's better for wing joints, tail sections and those fuselage upright to longeron joints where twisting is more likely. White glue is good around nose areas, wing and tail platforms, wing tips and landing gear supports where impact is more likely. White glue is a bit more brittle than Acetone and excess globs are harder to remove.

Gluing: Instant Glue

Cyanoacrylate or "Instant" glues certainly have many applications, but for the builder of rubber powered models the wood sizes involved don't provide adequate surface area for strong joints to develop. Even the gap filling types require a fairly good fit of the surfaces to be joined and in a 1/16" square strip there's not much room for error. Also, these glues penetrate so quickly that it's hard to position your stick before the glue sets.

There is one area, however, where I have found that the "Cyano" glues really excel. The "Lamination" section shows how to make wing tips, whole tail outlines and other areas with thin strips of Basswood bent around a fence of pins using instant glue.

Of course, instant glue is indispensable for field repairs. Some caution is indicated in the use of "Accelerator" for this type of glue. I found myself to be allergic to it and suffered some dizziness. A pinch of baking soda on the joint will do the trick. Carry a small amount in your field box. Also, instant glues can be used to "tack" a joint for later gluing. Metal-to-metal or metal-to-wood joints seem to hold well with instant glue. One of the best uses I have found for instant glue is the "Case Hardening" of balsa. A thin skin spread *fast* with your finger will harden the surface of balsa. This works really well in areas that have lots of wear such as nose blocks, wing tips, wing platforms and landing gear supports. Make several thin applications then dig your fingernail into the surface to check the hardness.

Gluing: Epoxy

Last, epoxy is a very underrated material. Many modelers avoid it because they have to mix two parts instead of just squeezing some out of a tube. Actually, epoxy is not only easy to use, it offers several times the strength of any other glue and will attach metal-to-metal or metal-to-wood making a joint that is impervious to almost anything. Where other glues lose weight as their solvent dries out, with epoxy what you put on is what you get so use it sparingly. I use epoxy wherever I need extreme strength, as in a prop assembly where I want to attach a blade to the hub or around the Dethermalizer snuffer tube. Wooden propeller tips get a lot of abuse and a carefully spread coat of epoxy helps here, but be sure to re-balance afterward. Epoxy will hold many plastics that other glues fail with. Also, I use it around all the small hooks that hold wing, tail, nose block and the half dowels or small hardwood keys I use to position wings and tail.

Sanding

I think any experienced modeler will tell you that his sanding block is his best tool. Good sanding technique is simple, materials are readily available and the results are well worth the effort.

You should have at least three different grades of sandpaper already attached to blocks. There are many refillable sanding blocks available and all do a good job. Any block is better than none. Start with 120 grit then 220 for most jobs. 400 and 600 grit will handle your final finishing work. It's also nice to have a sanding block with a couple of rounded edges of different sizes to handle fairings and corners.

The secret to good sanding is a light touch and a lot of strokes. Never press hard on the block. Let the grit do the work. When you can, stroke away from you (Fig. 3-5), holding the material on the board to avoid catching and breaking the wood as you pull towards you. In kits that

FIG. 3-5. Sand away from you.

have die cut sheet parts a good idea is to sand the back of the sheet with 220 grit to help release the parts. A long piece of aluminum extrusion will help in sanding finished wings and fuselages. Try to avoid using sandpaper in your hand with no backing blocks. That's another quickie solution that usually takes longer to correct. There's no way you can sand evenly with a small piece of paper in your hand.

Leo McCarthy suggests gluing a 12″ x 12″ sheet of 120 to one side of a piece of ¾″ ply and a sheet of 240 to the other. The sheet on the bottom will hold the board still while you sand your model part by moving *it* across the board. This is very good for wing bottoms and fuselage sides.

Buy a "Tack Rag" in your local paint store and use it to lightly wipe off the surface you have sanded, then hold the part or sheet at an angle to a strong light and sight along the surface. Any dents or parts you missed will quickly show up. If you want to be really exact, sprinkle a little talcum powder on the surface then scrape very lightly with the edge of a playing card along the surface. Most of the talc will wipe off but it will remain in any depressions and hang up around any bumps. Just make sure you wipe away all the talc before doping.

4

Sheet Balsa Construction

As we did in an earlier chapter, let's start learning about sheet balsa construction by building a model. The Canarsie Courier is the next step in our program and adds a pylon, landing gear and an airfoiled wing to our basic design getting us close to real performance. The Courier can do one minute or better in calm evening air and is extremely durable.

To build the Courier we should add some more tools. Various types of clamps (Fig. 4-1) will help in assembly. A building board is now a must. Lumber yards sell a material called "Homesote" that works well. Guillow's sells a very fine, flat balsa building board. Soft pine will do but corrugated cardboard will not. You need something that will allow you to push pins in easily yet will hold them firmly and will not warp.

In the Courier plan (Fig. 4-2), we find some new expressions: TYP. means that this dimension or part repeats in several places. DOTTED LINES indicate that you are seeing the edge of the part *through* another thickness of balsa (see ribs in top view of the wing). SEPARATE VIEWS are shown to simplify building. The wing is shown as seen from above while the fuselage is seen from the side. DETAIL PARTS are shown separately. Note that the wing rib appears 3 times. Once in full size, once at the top of the pylon in half size, and once on the fuselage side view in ¼ size. All three of these views of the rib are dimensioned so you can learn to scale plans from this book or a magazine to full size. Just note the measurements between points A,B,C,D,E on each view and compare them to the actual sizes. Most of the plan is ¼ scale. That is, the drawings are ¼ the size of the actual model. If you measure each part and multiply by 4 you will get the true size. DIMENSIONS are duplicated on several plans in this book to aid the beginner in learning to scale.

Start by choosing a sheet of 1/32" x 3" balsa, medium hard with very

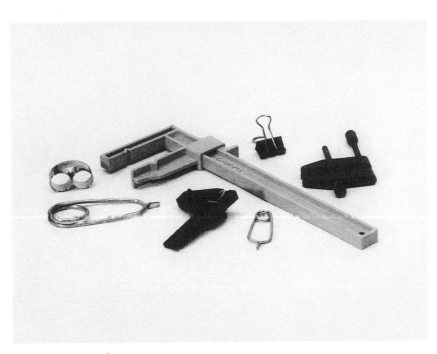

FIG. 4-1. Various clamps.

straight grain. Cut a piece 18″ long for the wing and draw a ball point line (press hard as the wing is meant to be cracked along this line) 18″ long and 1″ in from the leading edge. Next, *VERY LIGHTLY* draw lines from L.E. to T.E. at 4½″, 9″ and 13½″. Cut another piece 1/32″ x 1″ x 18″ and glue it to the wing to double the thickness for the first inch back from the Leading Edge. This should be on the opposite side from your ink line. Cut the tip shape and the notches where the ailerons will go. Now with the extra piece on the bottom, use a straight edge to crack the wing towards you at the ink line.

Cut four ribs as shown from medium to hard 1/16″ sheet. Take two of these ribs and tack them together lightly along the bottom with a spot or two of glue at two points while inserting a small piece of 1/8″ balsa at the high point. These will be your center ribs and will create the correct dihedral angle. This is a bit hard to visualize so study Figs. 4-2 and 4-3 carefully before assembling ribs to the wing. The ribs on your plan have been extended 1/8″ on their bottoms to increase strength. *This does not show on the sketches.*

Correct dihedral angle is very important as your models get larger and heavier. A small difference from one wing to the other can result in the

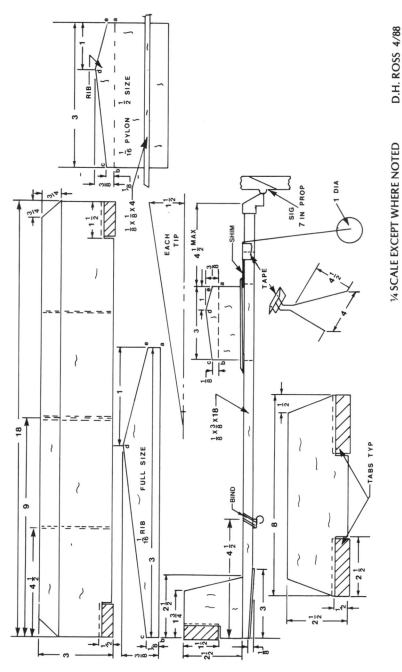

FIG. 4-2. Canarsie Courier

22

dreaded death spiral.

With the extra 1″ x 18″ piece on the bottom, glue and pin all the ribs to the rear 2″ of the wing. Carefully align the double center rib along your ink line and glue it in too. Try bending up the front of the wing while all this is pinned in position to make sure all ribs fit and line up perpendicular to the span. After the ribs are thoroughly dry remove the pins and tilt the rear up so the front 1″ is flat on the board then glue the ribs to it. I have shown the wing in both stages in the figures.

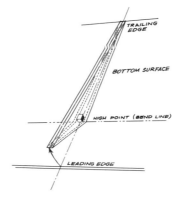

FIG. 4-3. Assembly of center ribs with ⅛″ spacer.

After the wing is thoroughly dry, remove it from the board and insert a razor between the two center ribs along their base. Cut them apart and continue the cut as shown right through the wing center. You will note that the wing overlaps the edges of the center ribs at the tops. Place the wing at the board or table edge with the tip blocked up 1½″ and sand away this excess as shown. Continue sanding until the face of the rib matches the wing and is smooth. If you find this method difficult, make 1/8″ thick (or laminate two 1/16″ pieces) center ribs, cut the wing in half at the 9″ line, glue the 1/8″ ribs square at the center and sand in the dihedral angle with a 1½″ block as shown in Fig. 4-4.

Now you can cut the pylon from hard 1/16″ balsa taking care that the grain is vertical. Note that the top of the pylon is shaped just like a wing rib. The pylon is glued between the two center ribs and pinned in place (Fig. 4-5). The next operations will make your model more stable and durable. Cut a piece of gauze, nylon or cotton cloth, (I keep a stock of discarded panty hose material) and with a liberal dose of glue, work it into the top of the wing at the dihedral joint. Cut a piece of hard 1/8″ square x 4″ long and glue it to the right side of the pylon as shown. This

23

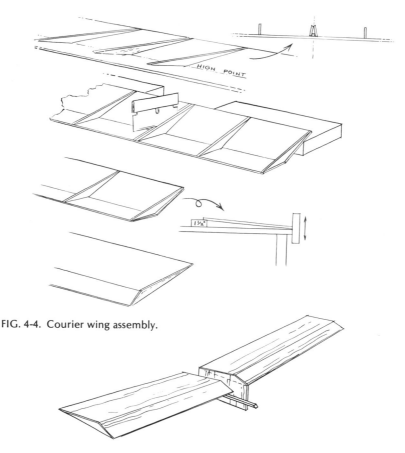

FIG. 4-4. Courier wing assembly.

FIG. 4-5. Pylon & wing halves.

allows you to attach the pylon to the motor stick with rubber bands so it can absorb a crash and so you can adjust the wing for flight trim. Run a heavy bead of glue along the inside and outside of the wing at your 1″ ink line to strengthen the cracked area.

The motor stick is a hard piece of 1/8″ x 3/8″ with the rear 2½″ tapered from the bottom as shown on the plan. Take care when making this taper cut to hold the knife as square as possible so the stab will not tilt.

The rest of the construction is standard. Glue the rudder to the right side of the motor stick and the stab to the bottom making both as square as possible. Bend the 1/32″ landing gear wire as shown then fold a piece of masking tape over it so it sits on the motor stick like a saddle. This will allow you to hold the landing gear on with a rubber band.

Removable landing gear is a big help in balancing a model, packing it for transit or changing it into a zippy hand launch.

Bend a wire hook for the rear of the motor stick and bind with thread and glue. Put on some stiff paper tabs as shown, attach the pylon to the left side of the motor stick and make a rubber motor of one loop of 3/16" x 16" long. Move the pylon and landing gear back or forward until the model balances at the center of the wing. You should color trim with magic marker before balancing. If you want to do some really fancy color trimming do it while all the parts are in the flat sheet form before construction. A little careful planning will keep your trim lines away from areas that will be cut, glued or sanded. A neat way to trim is to outline the color areas with a ball point pressed lightly into the wood. Use a contrasting color or the trim color. The ball point line will keep most magic marker inks from "bleeding" past your color boundaries.

Using colored paper trim tabs will add to the visibility of your model because this one can go really high. Do not dope the Courier but keep it away from dampness. The Courier will fly well indoors or out with 3/16" rubber. Also, you might try 1/16" wood for the wing, delete the extra leading edge piece and build the wing by one of the other methods shown. With the extra wing and tail thickness you can now apply two thinned

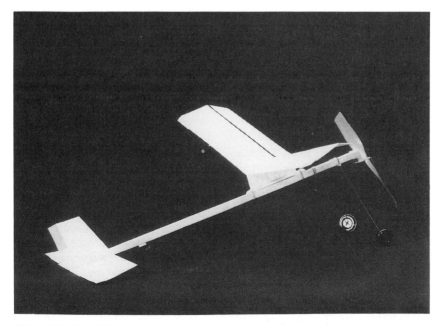

FIG. 4-6. Finished Courier.

(50-50) coats of dope and have a real outdoor model. Put your name on this one—it can fly away.

If your Courier will not climb under medium power, try adding a 1″ piece of 1/16″ x 1/8″ balsa between the bottom front of the 1/8″ square wing hold down and the top of the fuselage. This is called an "Incidence Shim" and is shown on the plan. Also, remember to check the prop bearing for wobble.

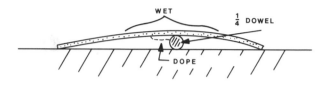

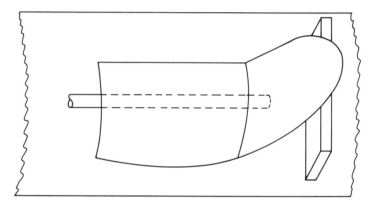

FIG. 4-7. Dowel Method.

Sheet Balsa Wings

Two "ribless" wing construction methods are shown. The dowel idea is about the lightest and simplest, a bit tricky to build but worth the trouble. My 49'er *(Model Builder '72)* has been flying for ten years with just a few dents. Cut the wing outline and the dihedral breaks. Lightly dope the center inch of the bottom and wet the top. Bend one section over a ¼″ dowel or pencil and tape down. By the "cut-and-try" method, sand and fit the other sections to make a perfect joint. Glue and re-inforce with tape (Fig. 4-7). This type is very strong and warp resistant yet very light. My 49'er spent two rainy days in a tree and showed no warps.

The other "ribless" type was developed by Woody Blanchard for his "Poco" .020 gas design (AM '58) and is incredibly simple yet strong and a good flyer. Simply block up a sheet of 1/16″ or 1/32″ on 1/16″ strips then sand and assemble two lengths of tapered trailing edge stock so they

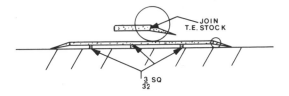

FIG. 4-8. Poco wing.

droop at front and rear (Fig. 4-8).

The "Jedelsky" method is clear from the sketch and is used on heavier models (Fig. 4-9).

The notch sander shown in Fig. 4-10 A&B can be one of your most useful tools. Make one each for 1/16" sq., 1/16" x 1/8" and 3/32" sq. and you will cover the range. Just glue a strip of hardwood or hard balsa of the size required to a 2" wide piece of 1/8" sheet about 6" long. Carefully cut a strip of 220 grit sandpaper to the width required (not as hard as it seems) with a straight edge and a new blade and glue the paper to the strip. Sand lightly across the rib and the strip will cut its way right in to the correct depth.

Sheet Fuselage

A very square sheet balsa fuselage can be made by pre-cutting 1/16" x 1/8" cross pieces in sets of two (top and bottom) then use the notching tool with both sides pinned together. Glue in the center set of four cross pieces, block the sides up very square until dry then pull in front and rear of the sides and glue in the rest of the cross pieces. See Fig. 4-11.

Before we go any further into construction, let's talk a bit about weight. Since weight is almost a direct trade-off with flight duration, and strength and weight are major factors in durability, the case for all balsa models is a good one.

I weighed several types of all sheet models and found in all cases that the wing loading (grams per sq in of wing area) for rubber models up to 30" span was well under the maximum of .5 gms/sq in. All came out within 20% or better of built up models of the same type and were a lot stronger.

Since sheet models can be built so much faster than built up types, they make wonderful test beds for new designs or tryouts for unusual scale types. It's tough to spend a lot of time building a model of a canard or flying wing then find out it is virtually untrimmable without major design changes.

Wing Area

Wing area mentioned above is probably the single most important

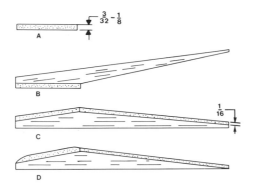

FIG. 4-9. Jedelsky wing.

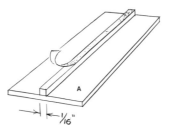

FIG. 4-10A. Notching tool.

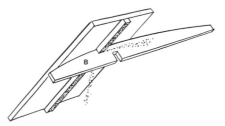

FIG. 4-10. Wing rib being notched.

number you need for building, trimming or designing models. In most models the wing is carrying all of the model weight. The fuselage is just there to house the motor and prop and connect the wings with the tail group which adds stability and control. To find if the wing can carry its load we need to be able to calculate its area. This is simple on a rectangular wing. Area is span times chord. To get the area of all other wing shapes we need only two more simple rules and a very small bit of ingenuity. The two rules are: a) the area of a right triangle is the height times the width, divided by 2 and, b) the area of a semi-circle is (Pi x R x R)/4 where Pi is 3.1414 and R is the radius of the circle at the tip.

Fig. 4-12 illustrates the worst case.

28

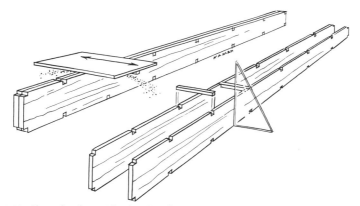

FIG. 4-11. Sheet fuselage sides for Condor.

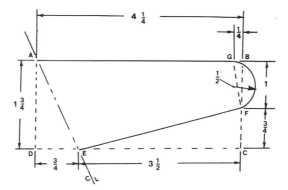

FIG. 4-12. Wing area calculation.

The actual wing is marked with wood grain lines and is defined by points A,E,F and G plus the rounded tip. We solve the problem by turning the wing into a rectangle A,B,C,D, whose area is 1¾" x 4¼" = 7.437 sq in. Now add the area of the tip: 3.1414 x ½" x ½" all divided by 4 = .196 sq in. The total of these two is 7.633 sq in.

Now we subtract the areas of triangles A,D,E and E,C,F which are: 1¾" x ¾" divided by 2 = .656 sq in and 3½" x ¾" divided by 2 = 1.313 sq in. We must also subtract the area of the small triangle FGB because we already counted that in the area of the tip. This is ¼" x 1" divided by 2 = .125 sq in. The three triangles add up to 2.094 sq in. Subtract this from 7.633 sq in. to get 5.539 sq in. This is the area of *ONE* wing. Double this for the total area of 11.078 sq in. This is a figure we will use for many other calculations besides wing loading. We will need it to help choose a prop size and to decide on a Center of Gravity (Balance Point) location for many different types of models. The case above was the worst I could imagine. Most of your area calculations will be simple and can be approximated quickly.

29

FIG. 4-13. Don Ross's 24" all sheet 49'er.

FIG. 4-14. Don Ross's 22" all sheet scale "Sperry Messenger."

5

AMA Racer

Before going on to stick and tissue construction, a very fine transition model is the "AMA Racer." Costing about $1.50 from Sig, this little 18" span beauty illustrates not only how to glue sticks and paper but can also be used to learn the rudiments of free flight trimming.

The kit as it comes makes a fair flyer. With only a few small modifications though, it can break one minute indoors and catch thermals outside. Also, the kit is very cleverly designed to introduce the beginner to stick and tissue construction. The plan is printed on a very thin, light, onion skin type paper. The model is built by actually gluing the sticks to the plan which becomes the covering when it is cut out. Fig. 5-1 shows the completed Racer with tabs added.

First, cut the ⅛" x ⅜" motor stick to ⅛" x ¼" except where the prop

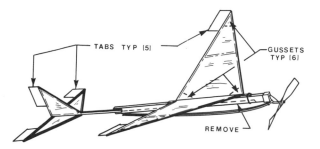

FIG. 5-1. AMA Racer with modifications.

hanger requires the extra width. Use a hard piece of 1/16" x 1/8" balsa for the tail boom and incline it 1/8" at the rear end. Add 1/16" thick gussets at the three corners of each wing and add five tabs made from stiff construction paper as shown. The tabs should be about 1" wide and extend ½" to ⅜" beyond the trailing edge. The tabs can be bent up or down (or sideways on the rudder) singly or in pairs to produce turns, climbs, etc. The chapter on flight trimming covers this in detail but a lot of fun at low cost along with some painless learning is available in those few sticks and a bit of rubber. One loop of ⅛" rubber 12" long wound to 500 turns is all the power you will need.

When balancing the Racer, don't move the wing front more than 1½" from the nose. If the wing needs to be moved further back, add some clay to the nose.

6

Built-Up Stick Model

I strongly believe the three previous steps are necessary even for the modeler who has had some experience with kits or "scratch building" (building from plans). Without proper guidance it's very easy to start down the wrong path and form some bad building habits. Now, however, the path splits. Before starting a real stick and tissue model I suggest something like the Sig Cub. At 24" span with built up wing and tail and a strong stick fuselage, this is almost a competition model. The plans are quite complete and include movable control surfaces on the tail and wire landing gear for ROG (Rise Off Ground). The wing is movable and tiltable and at $4.25 you have a swell test bed for rubber and even CO_2.

Again, I suggest modifications. Aileron tabs on the wing and an adjustable prop hanger (see prop chapter) add some fine tuning. A larger prop later on and you may have a thermal hunter.

Another approach to transition is the "Canarsie Condor." I designed this to provide an attractive sport model with good performance and simple construction techniques. The plan shows the layout and dimensions. The next chapter discusses the building techniques in detail. Read them while building the Condor.

Durations of over a minute are easy with the Condor and there's nothing quite like the thrill of seeing the structure silhouetted through the tissue against the evening sky.

The plan is shown in Figs. 6-1 and 6-2 with wing details in Fig. 6-12 and a "bare bones" picture in Fig. 6-32.

The basic fuselage construction was covered in Chapter 4 and shown in Fig. 4-11. Dimensions of the Condor fuselage are shown above and below the center line at points A,B,C. These are used in scaling by first

33

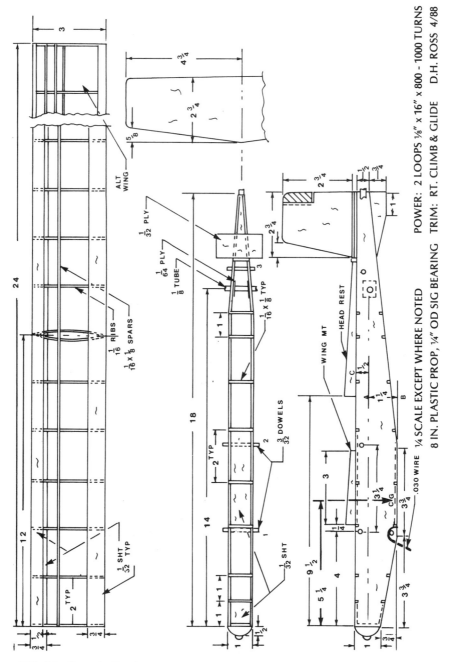

FIG. 6-1. Canarsie Condor.

Table 6-1. Beginner's Built-Up Models.

20-24 In. Span Simple Construction, Good Flyers:	
Comet - Cloud Buster	Micro-X - Hornet
Easy Built - Baby Flea	Peck - Moth
Fresno - Oriole Jr.	Sig - Tiger
Guillows - Javelin	Schleuter - Pacific Ace
P-30:	
Blue Ridge - Square Eagle	Peck - One Nite 28
Campbell - Souper	Pharis - Potent RN - Panda
Advanced Models 30 In. And Up:	
Comet - Sparky	Fresno - Miss Worlds Fair
Guillows - Arrow	RN - Korda, Maverick, Sparrowhawk

laying out a center line then measuring above and below it at critical points, multiplying these dimensions by the scale factor and laying out these new values on your sketch in the same locations. For instance, dimension A-B measures 5/16″ on your plan. Since the scale is ¼ we multiply 5/16″ by 4 to get 1¼″ then place this on our sketch. Try the same thing with dimension A-C. Both show true measurements on the plan top to help you. Other dimensions are duplicated to help the beginner in visualizing and scaling. Again we use wiggly lines to show grain, dotted lines to indicate that the surface is behind or below another surface. Note that dowels "1" and "2" show dotted because they are under the top fill-in sheet but dowel "3" as well as the aluminum tube, shows full because they are in clear view. Ribs show dotted only when they pass under the sheet strip at front and rear. A careful study of the alternate wing structure compared with the rib will show you which spars pass over the rib and which pass under.

Both top and side views of the fuselage appear. Now you can follow lines down from the top view to points on the side. The dowels are a good example. Note that the head rest is omitted from the top view.

The full sized ribs are shown in what is called a "Section View." This is the picture you would see if you sliced the wing through the center of the rib. The cross hatched areas are the end grain of the spars or the sheet L.E. (leading edge) and T.E. (trailing edge).

The stabilizer stop is part of the D.T. (dethermalizer) mechanism described later. It is just a ⅛″ square strip glued to the fuselage top for the stab to pivot on.

Note that the dimensions shown for the wing rest are *CRITICAL*. They must be as exact as you can make them to insure that the wing rests evenly and at the correct incidence angle.

A good tool to start with here is a balsa stripper like the Jim Jones one shown in Fig. 6-3. This will provide uniform spars or longerons.

35

The rest of this chapter will combine instructions for the Condor with conventional stick and tissue construction.

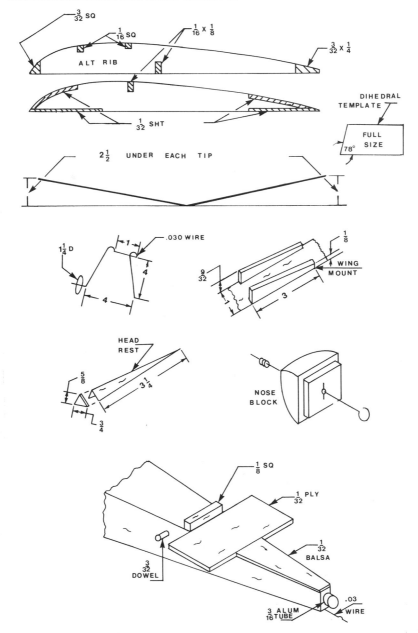

FIG. 6-2. Condor details.

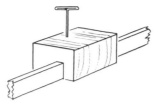

FIG. 6-3. Clamp block made with notching tool.

Construction

Careful attention to the basic techniques of stick and tissue construction will not only make your model look and fly better, it will last a lot longer too. Many a contest has been lost or a sport model wrecked because a critical joint cracked or slipped.

There's no magic in good craftsmanship, nor is special talent required; just a willingness to take the time to use the tools properly.

Since most builders start with the fuselage, so will we. Study your plan carefully the night before you start. Decide if you would like to photocopy parts of it so you can cut them up for easier mounting on your board. Make sure to compare several dimensions between the original and the copy before starting, copying machines often distort. Tape your plan to the board as smoothly as you can then tape over it a tight layer of Saran wrap. Wax paper will do but I have found the wax sometimes gets into a glue joint and weakens it.

Here's where we start selecting the best wood for each purpose as we discussed in an earlier chapter. Your longerons are the main fuselage structural members and must support the entire airplane in flight. They hold the wing and tail in alignment and absorb the twist and tension of the rubber and the impact of any crashes. They must not only be strong they must be as equal as possible. If you have stripped these all from the same sheet, you can be pretty sure they will be the same. The Jim Jones balsa stripper has the ability to spot hard areas on a sheet so it can be a help in making sure all your strips are the same. I generally choose "A" grain for longerons when I use balsa, but, for all models 30" span and over I have been using bass strips. This allows me to use a smaller strip (3/32" sq. instead of 1/8") and provides a lot more strength with almost no weight penalty. Good bass sheet and strip is available at hobby shops that carry model railroad supplies. It also comes in shapes like "I" or "U" beams that may be interesting to try.

If you use strip stock then test several sticks until you get four that are as alike as practical. Fig. 2-1 showed a simple test procedure or you can hang a small (1 oz.) weight on the end of each strip and pick the four that bend the least.

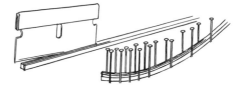

FIG. 6-4. Slit longerons before bending to prevent cracking.

Once you have your longerons, test for uprights the same way except they need not be as hard or stiff. Eight to 10 lb. balsa is best for longerons while 6 lbs. is OK for uprights and will save a little weight.

At this point you may want to cut your uprights to size against the plan before the longerons get in the way. I usually cut two at once to be sure they are identical in length. The portable chopper can be laid right over the plan as shown. Next begin to pin down the longerons. *NEVER* pin through the wood of *ANY* part of your model. I use a variety of pins for different purposes. Freeborn Enterprises makes some dandy pins in several sizes with big, cylindrical heads that serve well to hold parts down to the board. Fig. 6-3 shows a simple clamp block you can make using your notching tool. A few of these in each size will save a lot of work and help true up all your construction.

Some plans call for deep or sharp bends in longerons, particularly near the nose. Soaking in water with a few drops of ammonia will soften the wood so it will bend without cracking. Also, you might try several cuts in Fig. 6-4. Splices may be needed when you don't have a long enough stick. Always make a long diagonal splice, never a sharp butt cut. Wherever your longeron is bent or curved, use plenty of pins to support the bend. Pin closely on both sides and this will help prevent cracking. If you do crack one, replace it, don't try to save it. That will reduce warps and twists. Fig. 6-6 shows a fuselage section including clamp and gussets.

When using Acetone glue, I double glue all uprights. This is not necessary with white glue. When using hardwood longerons and balsa uprights you should use white glue.

When the first fuselage side is complete, allow at least 2 hours for drying. This is an assembly that *must* be solid and square. There are several ways of building a duplicate second side. Some prefer building right on top of the first side then cutting the two apart with a double edged blade slid carefully between. Some build both together by pinning two longerons to the board, one over the other then slitting the assemblies apart. I have been successful in removing all the pins but not lifting the side off the board. It will stay firmly stuck to the Saran. Now lay a second sheet of Saran over the top and replace the pins as you add the second set of longerons and glue the uprights. If you take extra care at

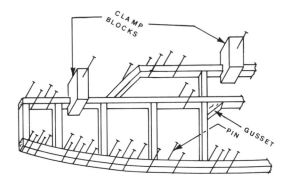

FIG. 6-5. Fuselage side.

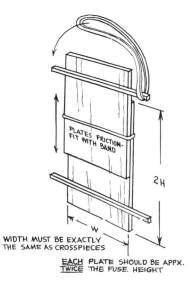

PLATES FRICTION-FIT WITH BAND

2 H

W

WIDTH MUST BE EXACTLY
THE SAME AS CROSSPIECES

EACH PLATE SHOULD BE APPX.
TWICE THE FUSE. HEIGHT

FIG. 6-6. Fuselage squaring jig.

this point, the two sides will be identical.

If any of the pre-cut uprights do not fit properly, discard and cut another set. Forcing a part too tightly will result in strains that lead to warps. Trying to use a short piece is just as bad. The glue that fills in the gap will shrink as it dries and will also produce strains. A good fit is one where the two parts will stay together by themselves and not be so tight the wood bends. A square butt end is, of course, very important.

While your sides are still pinned down, a word about warping. Some builders of larger models spray the flat assembly (wing, stab or fuselage) lightly with water and allow it to dry overnight. They feel this removes the internal strains and "sets" the wood against future warps. I have tried this and noticed that models so treated never show warping even after being rained on. However, for the beginner, I think properly fixturing the parts while the paper is shrunk will do the job.

After removing the sides from the board, cutting away glue globs and lightly sanding the inside faces, you are ready to assemble. Study the plan and pick four cross pieces that would outline a square cornered box in the fuselage. These will probably be right under the wing. Some scale models may not have such an area so choose somewhere about the middle where the wing sits. Cut all your cross pieces as you did the uprights and put aside the four that cover your base area. Make sure top and bottom cross pieces are identical unless shown differently on the plan.

Most fuselages will have a flat spot in the same area as your base. This may be on top or bottom. If there is no flat spot, block up the sides with scrap so they sit firmly on your board. All you need here are a few blocks of ½" or ¾" soft balsa cut into right angle triangles about 2" x 3". These have innumerable uses in creating square glued joints. Block up the two sides and allow the glue to dry thoroughly. Another method for squaring up sides is the "H" frame. Make two identical ones out of scrap (Fig. 6-6). The fuselage inside width must be exact but the height can be adjustable. Attach with rubber bands as shown to hold the sides in perfect alignment while they dry (Fig. 6-7).

After the sides are dry, cut 12 to 24 small gussets from 1/16" hard sheet. The gusset should cover three times the width of the joint and the grain should run parallel to the diagonal. The "Chopper" is a good tool for making continuous gussets from a strip simply by using the 45 degree stop and turning the strip over after each cut. These gussets are your insurance that the fuselage, and therefore the rest of the model, will stay square and in alignment. If every corner of the base box was gusseted,

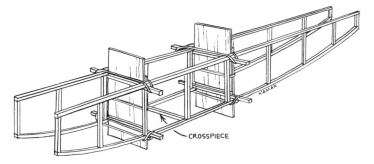

CROSSPIECE

FIG. 6-7. Squaring jig in position.

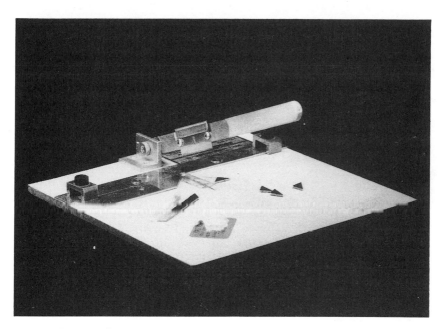

FIG. 6-8. "Chopper" tool for gussets, etc.

you would need 24 gussets. I usually use 8 on models up to 24" span and 16 on the larger ones. Don't leave the gussets out. They bear only a tiny weight penalty but a really big share of the stress and impact loads. The Chopper and some gussets are in Fig. 6-8.

Once the gussets are dry you can pinch the tail section together and add the nose cross pieces. A scrap block the size of the inside nose area is a help in squaring it up. Exacto makes some nice clamps that help here. I balsa fill the nose areas of all models to at least 1" back.

Now, you are about to get the first of many thrills in your modeling career. Hold the fuselage horizontally and look through from front to rear. Isn't that beautiful? It should combine the grace of the Eiffel Tower with the technological achievement of the Sydney Bridge. Your eye will be able to spot a misalignment of less than 1/64" so don't be upset if a stick or two is a hair out. Look for a "Banana" shape or a few corners that aren't 90 degrees. Make all the corrections required, test the joints for strength by wiggling lightly and look the whole thing over for areas that might need some extra support. Wing and stab platforms, rudder rests, landing gear braces, rear rubber holders and dethermalizer snuffer tubes are good places to check. Decide now where you are going to put your wing, tail and nose block retaining hooks or dowels. All these places should get some sheet balsa support even if the plan doesn't show it. Use

FIG. 6-9. Tail showing stab platform, wire & snuffer tube.

1/32" or 1/16" medium balsa and try to arrange the grain so any crushing action will not be against the end grain where it can split it. I use 1/32" ply on any model 24" or larger to make a stabilizer platform. 1½" to 2" wide x ¾" will provide you with a stable platform that will allow you to adjust the stab incidence and will hold it in position (Fig. 6-9).

Another area that needs special attention is the nose. When the fuselage is complete and square, glue in a thin ply (1/32" - 1/16") nose former that is 1/8" smaller inside than the frame. This serves as a strong base for the nose block and helps make it a snug fit. Also, on larger models this former can be tapped with 2-56 thread in three places and small, headless nylon screws can be inserted. These screws are perfect for making small adjustments in thrust and can be held in place with a drop of glue (Fig. 6-10).

I like to make my landing gear removable. This can cut your transport box height in half and gives an extra ounce of shock absorption to the fuselage. Just bend as shown and pass over a dowel and hold with rubber bands (Fig. 6-11).

Condor Fuselage

The Condor Fuselage is sort of in between the all sheet and the built-up type. Assemble the same as shown in Fig. 4-11 except that the top and bottom are tissue covered where shown. Once your base square area is dry, pinch the tail together and glue, slip in your nose spreader scrap piece and glue in all the rest of the cross pieces. Add gussets to the center area, fill in the nose, add your stab platform, landing gear braces and wing support rails.

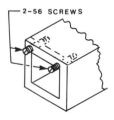

FIG. 6-10. Thrust adjusting screws in nose.

Wing Construction

This time let's start with the wing for the Condor. The secret to this wing is the *careful* cutting of the ribs. Use fairly hard 1/16" wood for these. I usually make a template of ply or thick cardboard for rib cutting. This way I get uniform ribs and easy extras to replace broken ones. Pin the ribs together in a stack and discard any that don't match. While still in the stack, notch all the ribs for the top spar.

Now pin down the 1/32" thick x ¾" wide strips at the front and rear of the wing. Lay the ribs on top making sure the notches fit right over the strips. Take care to pin the center ribs against the dihedral block. This angle insures proper dihedral and stable flight. Next, assemble the top spar and the top leading and trailing edge strips. These strips should touch each other at front and rear. When dry, remove from the board and sand with a wide block to make sure you have a smooth surface to cover. Fig. 6-12 shows the wing.

The Condor wing is somewhat heavier than a true stick and tissue

FIG. 6-11. Removable landing gear.

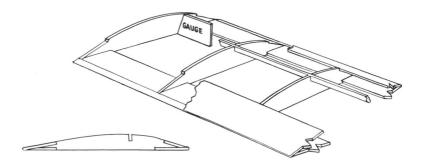

FIG. 6-12. Condor wing assembly.

wing but the small weight penalty is more than balanced by the strength to absorb the beginner's first flight tries.

Alternate Condor Wing

The alternate wing shown on the plan is built as described next. The rib is shown full size and is notched for the spars where shown.

Standard Wing

Construction of a standard wing is not much more complicated. Ribs are cut the same way. Leading and trailing edges are usually solid wood and are glued directly to the ribs. Many suppliers offer tapered trailing edge stock which is a real big time saver. If the builder wishes to make his own, the two dowel method is a help. Just pin your strip between two dowels of proper diameter, then carve and sand to shape (Fig. 6-13).

Your rib notching tool has still another use. Mark and notch your trailing edge for each rib. This will increase your warp and crack resistance tremendously (Fig. 6-14). Some plans call for the leading edge to be flat on the board and others show it a bit above the board in a "V" notch in the rib. If it should be raised, a few small scrap blocks will do the job. On my larger models I again use hard wood (bass) or the hardest balsa for the LE. These take the most punishment from strikes with fences, trees, cars, and such. Tony Peters uses a strip of Kevlar thread to armor his LE.

Wing spars should be a firm fit in the ribs and should lay straight along the wing. This may require some snipping and filing. Any gaps should be filled with scrap balsa, not glue.

When the model calls for undercambered ribs as shown in Fig. 6-15, you will have to block up each rib *AND* the front of the TE the proper amount to provide a smooth airfoil contour.

Before I discuss wing tips, bracing, etc., let's cover some other types of wing construction.

Sliced rib wings are very common in scale models. This is a means of saving weight and, also avoiding the layout job for each rib in a tapered wing. Sliced ribs are made from a template as shown. Simply mark your sheet with dots or lines every 1/16" or whatever height you require for a rib, then move the template down one line for each cut. As your wing tapers, just cut the back off each rib to fit. Sliced rib wings usually have a main spar which can be tapered from root to tip so the height of the airfoil diminishes towards the tip. Study Fig. 6-16. Just pin down your LE and TE and spar, then add ribs.

John Oldenkamp in his "Turkey" and "Crackerbox" designs has created an interesting variation on the sliced rib wing. Instead of slicing ribs for the top of the airfoil, his models simply use a piece of 3/32" balsa "cracked" with a fingernail at the proper place to cross the spar. Later, another thin spar is glued to the top of the cracked rib so the covering will produce a nice curve when applied. With an added Turbulator (discussed

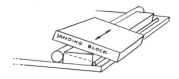

FIG. 6-13. How to make tapered trailing edges.

FIG. 6-14. Notched trailing edge.

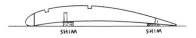

FIG. 6-15. Block up rib when assembling undercambered wing.

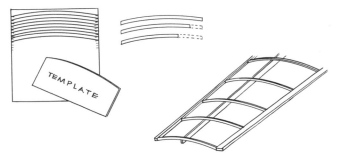

FIG. 6-16. Sliced rib wing.

later) I lost my Crackerbox OOS on a cold, damp fall day that no one would think could support thermals (Fig. 6-17).

For larger models I think the "Union Jack" method is the lightest and most warp resistant. As shown in Fig. 6-18, the ribs are criss-crossed in a geodetic design. The center rib is made in one piece and the side ribs are cut in half to fit. This is a bit harder to make than a multi-spar rib but worth the effort. Champion's "Upshot" and "Coupe" kits come with pre-cut geodetic ribs. Mine is six years old and still warp free.

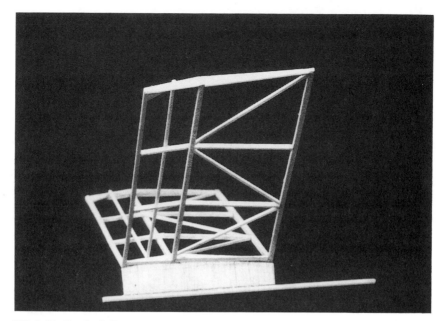

FIG. 6-17. Cracked rib wing.

Wing Tips

Wing tips are important to discuss. This is probably the one spot on a model that takes the most abuse and is hardest to repair. A crushed tip is hard to patch and often requires stripping the paper and rebuilding. Therefore, strong, light tips are essential.

Most plans show sheet tips made up of several pieces. This is not just to save wood. You should cut your sheet tips so the grain runs around the tip thus reducing chances of splitting or warping (Fig. 6-19).

Lately, many in our group have been using molded wood for wing tips and even tail group outlines. These are immensely stronger, a lot lighter and more warp resistant than sheet tips and are hardly more trouble to make. One method is to cut a thick cardboard outline of the tip making sure to factor in the thickness of your strips so the finished tip is not oversized.

Rub the edge of the template with a wax candle or crayon, soak your balsa strips (two or more thin ones are better than one thick strip) in water with ammonia and "pull" them around the template attaching with small strips of masking tape and gluing with white glue. Allow to dry thoroughly overnight, remove from the template and assemble to wing. A good rule for the beginner is to use 1/16" wood for wings up to

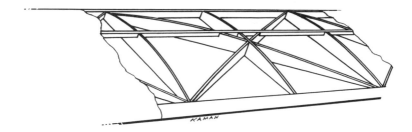

FIG. 6-18. Union Jack wing.

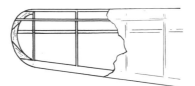

FIG. 6-19. Cut tips so grain follows curve.

1½″ wide, 3/32″ from 1½″ to 3″ and 1/8″ for larger wings. These wood thicknesses should always be more than one layer (Fig. 6-20).

Another method, credited to Paul Kaufmann is the hardwood lamination. This method eliminates the template and for larger models provides the strongest tips I've ever seen. Paul simply creates a fence of pins outlining the tip or the structural area he wants. Then he "pulls" thin strips (.015″ to .020″) bass around the curve and runs a bead of thin Cyano glue on top of the seam. The glue sinks into the joint by capillary action and in ten minutes you are ready to assemble. I've been using this method for the last five years on all kinds of models and it's interesting to note that I show up at our yearly One Design contest with all five of the previous models still in flyable condition. A finished tip made of hardwood is absolutely warp free. Tail group outlines also resist warp very well. If you use hardwood, you only need 1/2 to 2/3 the thickness of balsa. Joe Deppe will cut bass as thin as you want in many widths at good prices. Another small note about hardwood lamination. Later in this book we will discuss Profile or "No-Cal" models. Wing, tail and fuselage outlines can be made from two layers of .015 bass to provide strength with very little weight penalty and to avoid water soaking of balsa to bend around curves. I've actually saved weight on some models this way. Note that as you become more expert the wood sizes specified above can be reduced (Fig. 6-21).

Before assembling the wing in the flat, give some thought to how you

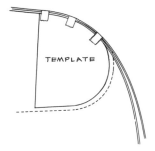

FIG. 6-20. Molded balsa tip on cardboard template.

are going to arrange the dihedral or polyhedral. Dihedral is the angle between a horizontal line and the bottom of a wing as seen from the front. Polyhedral is the same thing except the wing breaks in more than one place. Some dihedral is necessary for all free flight models since they must recover themselves from any bank or tilt to the side. Some scale models, in order to more faithfully reproduce the original, have very little dihedral. This makes them extremely hard to trim and erratic in flight. If you are designing your own model, one inch under each wingtip per foot of span is usual.

Your plan will show the dihedral or polyhedral breaks in the wing. If a single rib appears at these stations, do not glue it in. If a double rib is shown then you can tilt each rib at the correct angle so when mated together they will hold the wing correctly.

For those who are mathematically inclined, the angle between the rib and the bottom spar is the complement or 90 degrees minus the dihedral angle of the wing. Otherwise just tack glue the ribs to the LE and TE then final glue when setting the angle. Do not assemble any top spars at this time since they will have to be shortened to fit later on.

Assuming you have glued in your tips you can now remove the wing halves or quarters from the board and sand the dihedral angle into the LE and TE and bottom spars if any. Block the tip up as shown in the chapter on sheet balsa construction and sand lightly until the ends fit snugly when the wing is set in the correct dihedral position.

Washout

Now let's talk about something called "Washout" that you may see on magazine plans and will read more about in the Flight Trim chapter. Washout is a twist of the wing where the rear is slightly raised at the tip. The theory behind this is simple and may as well be covered at this point (Fig. 6-22).

Assuming constant speed, a wing will begin to "stall" or to lose lift as its angle to the approaching air (relative wind) increases. When the wing stalls the airplane falls out of the air until the nose drops, lowering the

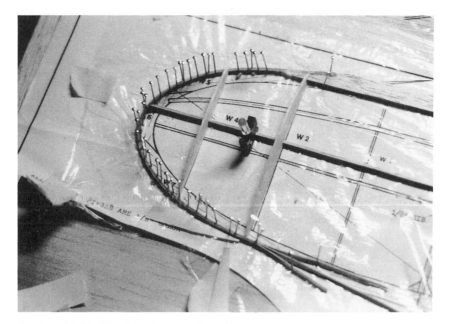

FIG. 6-21. Molded hardwood tip on plan using cyano.

wing angle and the wing picks up enough speed to again create lift. Unfortunately, the ground sometimes interferes too soon. Also unfortunately, all of the wing doesn't stall at the same time. If either tip stalls before the center then the model will bank, stall more and faster, then spin and crash.

Therefore, we try to twist the wing tip up at the TE so it is at a slightly lower angle with the fuselage reference line or the line of the relative wind (angle of attack) than the center. The tips will then stall later thus forcing the model to remain level.

Washout is much easier to do than to explain. Once you have sanded your LE, TE and spars to fit, create a fixture with balsa scrap so you can block up the wing tip and pin it firmly in place. While making your fixture, add a small shim under the TE. I use 1/16" from peanut to 24" span, 3/32" from 24" to 36", and 1/8" after that. I like to set up my wing

FIG. 6-22. Washout angle.

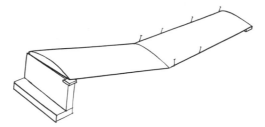

FIG. 6-23. Dihedral jig showing washout shims.

fixture on an extra board so I can leave it in place to hold the wing while the tissue shrinks after wetting and again after doping. This not only insures that the washout will remain, it prevents other warping as well (Fig. 6-23).

After the wing has dried thoroughly in the dihedral jig, you can add top spars, gussets and reinforcement. Good spar fits and gussets are really important on your wing. After all, the wing must carry all the rest of the airplane in flight. You may feel the wing is strong enough at rest but flying loads in a climb or a turn can easily flex and loosen poor joints. One of the things that distinguishes the expert from the novice is the expert's attention to these details. His models are easier to trim and fly more consistently because good joints and gussets keep them in the same alignment as when they left his board.

Gussets were discussed earlier and should be fitted on both sides of any dihedral breaks and where the end tip ribs meet the LE and/or the tip. Reinforcement is important and very simple to do. Household gauze or a piece of nylon mesh from a stocking makes fine bracing material. Just saturate it with glue then work it into the joint wherever you feel the wing might bend or crack.

After the glue dries, add another thin skin of glue and you will have a joint that is stronger than the surrounding wood. Look in your local phone book for someone who does Silk Screening and buy a few feet of his nylon mesh. This will last for years and cost only a dollar or two. Lastly, small gussets where the spars meet the tips greatly reduces tip crushing (Fig. 6-24).

FIG. 6-24. Re-inforce critical areas with silk or nylon.

Tail Group Construction

The tail group is much the same as the wing except that weight control here is more important than in any other part of your model. Since on most models, the tail is much further from the CG than the nose, weight at the tail counts more (it has a longer lever arm). Most models need nose weight for proper balance and every gram saved at the tail can save more than a gram at the nose, thus lighter tails are the way to lighter and better flying models. However, as in all engineering there's a trade-off to consider. The tail group, (rudder and stabilizer) pretty much control the flight path, therefore, we can't make them too weak or thin without risking warping or misalignment.

I have found that whole tail outlines made of thin, laminated hard wood come out lighter and much stronger than balsa assemblies. Most kits have print wood tail outlines. These should be used by the beginner but he can easily cut their width down to save some weight. In most cases, cutting the print wood to half its width and adding a few gussets at critical points will do the job. For Peanuts, I use balsa strips (1/20" or 1/16" sq.) soaked in water and ammonia and molded around a cardboard form.

As the models get larger, I begin to use multiple strips: two strips of 1/32" x 1/16" for 16-24" span; three strips of 1/32" x 3/32" for 25-36" span; and four strips of 1/32" x 1/8" for larger models.

Molded forms using thin hardwood have already been described. Bass as thin as .015" (1/64") can be used.

Again, gussets do an important job and should not be overlooked. Also, on some models it is useful to be able to move the control surfaces instead of the whole unit. Soft copper wire about .005" in diameter can be purchased in many hobby shops. Or you can strip some ordinary electric wire (I usually unplug it first!) and wind the strands together if too thin. Glue to each surface with epoxy or acetone glue and cover right over (Fig. 6-25).

Make sure that you strengthen the tail around any areas where rubber bands will pull or where it rests on the fuselage or where the dethermalizer mounts. These stress areas can easily distort a thin tail and destroy your

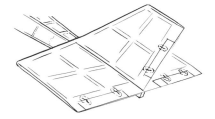

FIG. 6-25. Wire glued on as hinge for movable controls.

flight adjustments.

Rolled Balsa Tyvec Fuselage

The next item to discuss is a kind of fun way to build a fuselage for a sport or contest model. Some builders claim that these are "Bulletproof." I have found they are light, easy to make and will withstand a blown rubber motor with no protective tube.

First you need some "Tyvec." This is a fibrous material that is used to make the overnight mail envelopes used by the post office and many other mail and package services. You can often just pick up a few at your office. Also, Tyvec is now in popular use as a vapor barrier in wooden home construction. It comes in big rolls and any construction crew will probably let you have a few feet.

Tyvec is usually laminated to a paper base and can be split from that with a little careful work with a razor point and a tweezers. Lightly sand the fuzz off the Tyvec with 250 grit paper. Apply white glue, thinned 50-50, to the Tyvec, pin flat and allow to dry. Next select a sheet of A grain with the grain as straight as possible from 4-6 lbs. 1/32" balsa. The sheet should be 1/32" wider than the circumference of the tube you want to make. Circumference is 3.1414 times the diameter, or measure around your forming dowel with a piece of string. Use a dowel 1" to 1¼" diameter or a broomstick of appropriate size.

Sand the balsa lightly and apply thinned white glue to one side, pin down with glue side up and allow to dry overnight.

After both the balsa sheet and the Tyvec sheet are dry, place them with the glue sides together and iron over the Tyvec with a household iron on medium heat. The two surfaces will absolutetly weld themselves and the new conbination will begin to curl slightly towards the Tyvec. After the sheets cool, run them under a hot water faucet with the balsa on top. This will fill the wood with water causing it to swell and curl more around the Tyvec. As soon as the wood feels soft and pliable, bend it around your dowel and bind it tight. Ace bandage is much better than rubber bands here. Rubber bands tend to groove the soft balsa. A bit of silicone spray on the dowel under the balsa/Tyvec will help later in removing the

FIG. 6-26. Nose block retaining band.

finished tube.

Allow the combination to dry at least 24 hours on the dowel. Now slide the dry sheet off the dowel and glue the seam with Cyano as it comes off Spiral tissue wrap on the outside, put 1/16″ doublers at front and rear end and you have a motor tube that can weigh as little as 7 grams on a P-30.

Tyvec has many other uses on models. Laminated between two layers of thin balsa it makes strong prop blades, wheels, wing platforms and many other parts. It can be glued, doped and sanded and is proof against lots of solvents.

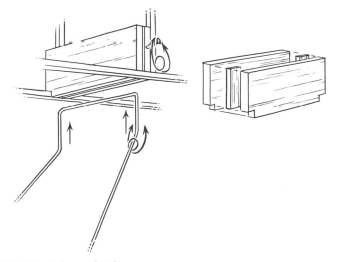

FIG. 6-27. LG in balsa sandwich.

MISCELLANEOUS CONSTRUCTION ADDITIONS

In order to disassemble your model for transport, re-assemble with the same adjustments and hold the adjustments throughout the various flight modes and crashes, you will need some hooks, dowels, platforms and locating keys. Many of these will be added after covering but their location points must be braced or sheeted at this stage. Let's start right at the nose and work rearwards to make sure we don't miss any.

Nose Blocks

Even with a tight fit, nose blocks work loose and when it happens in the air, disaster usually follows. Most modelers use a couple of hooks and a rubber band. Gene Scheppers drills a hole across the nose block just small enough to trap a knot in the rubber band he runs through the hole and over two hooks. If your nose block is tilted because of thrust adjustments, a tight rubber hold-in is even more important (Fig. 6-26).

53

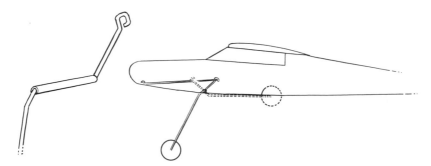

FIG. 6-28. Retractable landing gear.

Landing Gear

Next we have the landing gear. Fig. 6-27 shows a standard installation using a balsa sandwich. This is strong and light. Retracting gear is rather simple to make and adds a nice touch as well as improving the glide (Fig. 6-28).

On most of my models, the landing gear is removable. This allows smaller packages for traveling and permits changes in gear for larger props. Note that all these installations are braced and gusseted. Also, remember that wood cracks more easily parallel to the grain so set your bracing with the grain resistance in the direction that will take the most strain. I use soft "A" grain to fill in my nose areas and hard (8-10 lb.) "C" grain for bracing gussets and planking. When using the harder material you can go down a bit in thickness. If the longerons are 3/32", your hard gussets can be 1/16".

Wing Planforms

Wing platforms are next. Hard balsa with the grain spanwise is best. If the wing has an undercamber make sure the platform solidly supports the front and rear even if you have to carve some soft scrap curves to fit. Wing hold down rubber is held by dowels or wire hooks that must be solidly braced. *Never* place the dowels under the wing. They must be outside the wing chord to hold properly. Sometimes a single dowel pointing forward through the windshield is necessary. Also, the wing area that supports the rubber should be covered with thin, soft balsa under the tissue. Once the model is covered you are going to glue half dowels or small hard balsa keys at points on the LE and TE that will locate the wing against the platform (Fig. 6-29). These areas should be braced before covering.

You have probably already braced the fuselage area that supports the rear rubber peg. This should be 1/64" ply and can be glued on the inside.

Dethermalizers (DT's)

The stab and wing platforms are much alike except that the fuselage

FIG. 6-29. Half dowel wing locating keys.

gets quite narrow at the rear so you may require a 1/32" ply platform that extends to each side about 3/4" (Fig. 6-9). Here we need to do a little engineering because few kits or plans detail how to set up a Dethermalizer system. Believe me, any model that can get 50 feet high can disappear in a thermal. Rich Fiore once wanted to show me the glide on a new model. He gently launched it from shoulder height aiming at a point on the ground about 20 feet away. Before we could catch the model, with no power at all, it climbed to the top of an 80 foot tree and sat there grinning at us.

Basically, a dethermalizer is actuated by a timer or fuse to suddenly and drastically change the angle of the stab to around 45 degrees. This stops the plane in midair and causes it to descend slowly like a parachute—most of the time. That's why some modelers use D.T.'s that detach the wing entirely.

For this series, we will concentrate on the stab tilt D.T. We'll need a pair of hooks on top of the stab, hooks or dowel on the fuselage set so that the rubber band makes an angle of 45 degrees with the fuselage center line when it pulls the stab up, a stab pivot stop, and some way to stop the stab

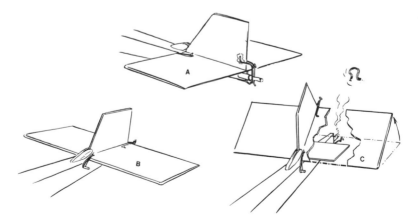

Fig. 6-30. A,B,C. standard DT operation.

travel. Also, on the rear of the stab we needed a wire to hold the fuse and small rubber band. On the fuselage rear, we have another wire to mate with the stab fuse wire and a snuffer tube to put out the fuse. Figs. 6-30A, B and C show the sequence.

For those models using a timer, the fuselage rear wire and snuffer tube can be eliminated. Some modelers prefer to mount the fuse in a more central location and run a cord to the rear. I think the best is Carl Goldberg's combination stab hook, stab locating wire and angle stop. When bent correctly in the Goldberg arrangement, no travel limiting cord is required. Fig. 6-13A & B show this sequence. For a weight penalty of less than 2 grams this is one of the best trade-offs you are likely to make in modeling.

The rubber bands used for DT's should be very thin so the fuse can burn through them easily. If you don't have access to a youngster who is undergoing orthodontia, try the smallest bands available in office supply stores. *DO NOT* double over a larger band. This may not burn through. Another source for DT bands is to cut some thin slices from the neck of a small balloon. Also note that in the sketch I show a small tube between the two hooks. This is called a "Snuffer Tube." The DT fuse is inserted in the 1/4" or 3/16" diameter aluminum tube and extends through the rubber band and out for whatever burn length you require. When it burns through the band, releases the DT action and reaches the snuffer tube, it goes out and prevents fire in dry areas. For larger models there are mechanical timers available that perform the DT fuse function. Also, there are several methods of modifying motors from "Tomy Toys" to act as timers. Both *Model Builder* and *Model Aviation* magazines published complete instructions for these modifications in their June 1982 issues.

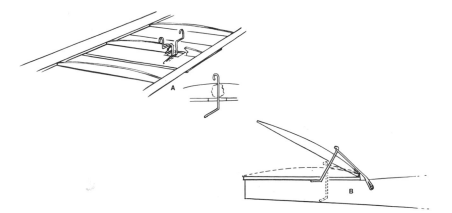

Fig. 6-31. A & B Goldberg DT.

Fig. 6-32. "Bare Bones" Condor to show construction.

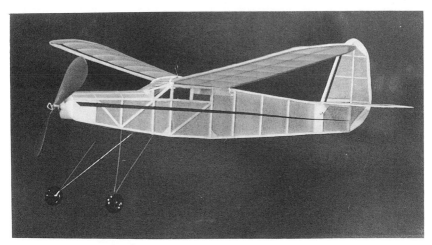

Fig. 6-33. Peck 24" "Moth" kit.

7

Covering

Covering gives a model its finished appearance, adds some strength to hold it together, and provides the surfaces which develop lift, stability and control. However as any experienced painter or woodworker will tell you, "A covering is only as good as the finish on the surface it covers." That's why sandpaper is the modeler's best tool.

You should have several grades of sandpaper from at least 120 to 400 and several blocks or sanding sticks. There are many sanding aids on the market and all do a decent job. First, take an Exacto knife and clean out all the glue globs at joints and corners. Then begin sanding with the 220 grit. Remember to sand with the grain wherever possible and don't press the sandpaper down on the work. Just slide it back and forth with minimal pressure and let the grit do the work. After the area feels smooth, go to the next grit and repeat. With light models we can't afford to seal the wood so we have to do our best with sanding. Your finger tips will tell you a lot about how smooth the work is. You can easily feel a difference of only a few thousandths of an inch in smoothness. Next, hold the work so the light runs along the surface and put it close to your eye. Tiny defects will show up quickly. If you need to fill in some areas, try Micro Balloons. Mixed with a little white glue they fill in the finest cracks and can be sanded smooth.

Of course, Peanuts and small scale models can't take a lot of sanding but you'll be surprised at how much good a bit will do.

Your sanding blocks should cover various shapes such as half rounds, square corners and concave curves. These can be made by buying shaped wood stock for ailerons, leading edges, etc. at a hobby shop or hard wood shapes from a railroad model supply store, and gluing sandpaper on with pressure sensitive cement.

Tissue

The tissue used for model covering is not the same tissue that you use to wrap Aunt Minnie's birthday gift. It weighs about half as much as ordinary store tissue and is a tighter weave so it will absorb less dope. Without proper care you can easily add 25% to the weight of your model by using the wrong tissue and poor doping technique.

Good tissue can be had from Peck, Champion, Old Time Models, Indoor Model Supply, FAI and others. For models up to 30" span, I use the lightest tissue I can get. At 30" I start using light (00) Silkspan for fuselages because I think the extra weight is a fair trade-off for the extra strength and easier covering. I use tissue on wings of all sizes.

Before starting to cover, check your tissue for grain direction. This can be done visually something like wood grain, or if you are not sure, tear a corner in both directions (Fig. 7-1). The direction with the grain will tear easily and in a straight line. Grain is important both for strength and sagging. If you have the grain wrong and the tissue sags between ribs, no amount of shrinking or doping will get it right. Once grain has been established, mark a corner with a small pencil arrow.

Tissue that has creases should be ironed. A dry iron on medium heat will take out folds and wrinkles right away. Although white tissue can be dyed I do not recommend this procedure for any but those with a very delicate touch. Tissue has almost no wet strength so you can easily rip it while dyeing.

We have already discussed careful sanding before covering. Next, it's not a bad idea to get a "Tack Rag" in a paint store to wipe all the sanding dust off your framework. No sealing is required before covering rubber models. The fuselage, however requires a bit of extra work because rubber lube somehow attacks glue joints and weakens them. Using a ¼" or ½" brush cover *all* of the fuselage structure where the rubber fits with a liberal coat of 50-50 dope.

Most builders today use Nitrate dope mixed 50-50 with thinner with a couple of drops of Castor Oil or Sig Retarder per ounce. I mix no more than 4 ounces at a time and use a slab of foam rubber around the base of the jar to keep it from tipping (Fig. 7-2).

A word here about brushes. Invest a few dollars in a set of the very best

Fig. 7-1. Tear tissue to spot grain.

Fig. 7-2. Keep dope bottle in foam block.

sable art brushes you can buy in ¼", ½" and 1" sizes. I have used the same brushes for over ten years in building perhaps 80-90 models and they are still like new. Using the best brushes will not only eliminate hairs in your dope coat, it will give you a more uniform job with less work. I simply wash each brush in thinner, wipe with a paper towel and coat with a dab of vaseline so air can't reach the bristles. I think it's the vaseline coat that does the job. This takes about 30 seconds per brush and works with colored of clear dope. I use a different brush for each color.

There are two basic methods of attaching tissue to your model. I prefer the dope method but Tony Peters and a lot of other fine modelers do just as well with thinned white glue.

Before starting to cover, plan out your tissue use so your are economical and don't get caught having to cover two sides of the fuselage with tissue from different sheets which may be slightly different colors. It's a good idea to save the scrap tissue from each job. Then at least you can patch with something close to the color you had at the start. Cut your tissue at least 1" oversized for each area. Note that dry tissue can't follow a compound curve so you will need an extra piece or small strips to cover the fuselage where it is round and also tapers. Wing tips also need a separate piece because the rib curves and the tissue dips down. Grain should be along the span of the wing and tail, and the length of the fuselage.

To use the white glue method, just mix the glue at least 50-50 with

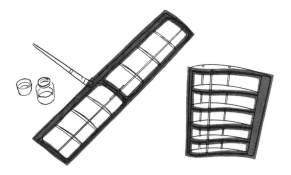

Fig. 7-3. Dope outside edges and undercambered ribs.

water, paint it on an area, and gently stretch the tissue over it while lightly rubbing it into the boundary sticks. You only put glue on the borders of the area you want to cover and you try, if practical, to work from the center towards each end.

Remember that tissue has no wet strength, so as soon as the water in the white glue touches it you start to feel the softening. I'm a little afraid of this method. My old, shaky hands tend to tear the tissue and somehow I feel all that water can't be helping the structure resist warping.

The dope method takes a bit more work and time but is less critical. First dope the outline of the area you want to cover with one coat of 50-50 (Fig. 7-3). Allow to dry overnight then sand *lightly* with 400 grit just to remove lumps. Now add another coat of 50-50 dope. For fuselages on larger models, I use three coats before covering. Remember, the outline of each section must be doped so don't forget the ribs at the dihedral breaks

Fig. 7-4. Flood thinner through tissue to dope underneath.

where you will use another piece of tissue, and the ends of the various fuselage sections. If the wing has undercamber, a bit of extra doping on the rib bottoms won't hurt.

Once the pre-doping is done and dry, set yourself up with a bottle of full strength dope, a bottle of thinner and a small brush. Now start applying the tissue as before except that you flood plenty of thinner *on top* of the tissue so it soaks through wherever you want it to stick down. Wait a few seconds for the thinner to soften the dope under the tissue and rub the tissue on to the wood. As you rub the tissue on, stretch it along its length and from side to side to get as wrinkle free an application as you can. You will learn very quickly just how hard your can stretch the tissue before it tears. If a piece is not going on so well, re-soften with thinner and try again. If a piece just won't stick, add some full strength dope in that area.

Wherever tissue must overlap at a seam, add a thin line of dope to insure good adhesion (Fig. 7-4).

Cover the bottoms of wing and tail structures first and the fuselage top and bottom before the sides. Don't worry if you still have some small wrinkles, we'll shrink them out later.

After covering an area (bottom of wing, top of fuselage), check from underneath or inside to make sure the tissue adheres to all the boundary sticks. Now is the time to touch up with a drop of full strength dope. This is particularly important on the bottom of undercambered ribs. I have even had to add some thinned glue to stubborn areas. These areas should be trimmed as close to the wood as possible. I use an ordinary emery board pulled across the edge. A sanding block will do as well but a razor blade tends to dig into the wood unless you have a very steady hand (Fig. 7-5).

After the bottom is covered and allowed to dry thoroughly, cover the top in the same general way, leaving at least a 3/4″ overlap. Wait for this to dry and trim carefully with scissors or a razor leaving about 1/8″ to 3/16″ overlap. Most builders like to overlap tissue at edges. This hides the bare wood and strengthens the covering without adding much weight. Working slowly this is easy to do using a brush, water and dope. Just wet the overlap with water, dope the edges you need and fold the wet tissue over and rub it in. On some edges like wing tips where the overlap tends to wrinkle because of curves, just cut some slits in it before folding and rub the extra layers in tightly (Fig. 7-6).

If you have used the white glue method I suggest that you place any parts that might warp into a fixture made from scrap while each tissue application dries. For the wing, use the original dihedral blocks and don't forget the washout shim. For flat stabs and rudders, pin them to a couple of 1/4″ square sticks which are pinned to your board. Warps are less likely to develop at this stage with the dope method.

After your tissue is applied and thoroughly dry, you will want to shrink

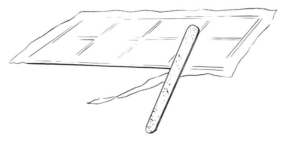

Fig. 7-5. Trim tissue with emery board.

62

it drum tight. Remember, though, that tissue has enough strength to bend thin wood. On Peanuts and other small models, tissue shrinking can be dangerous. Most builders of such models either don't shrink or dope the tissue at all, or employ one of several methods for pre-shrinking. To do this a frame of wood is built, the tissue taped to it, and water sprayed two or three times. It's possible to simply lay a tissue sheet down on newspaper and spray with water then iron flat when dry. Some builders even dope the tissue in the frame then carefully cover with strips to eliminate wrinkles.

Let's continue with our basic method at this time. Almost any means of depositing a fine mist of water on the tissue will do. Many hair spray dispensers can be refilled with water and used. A mixture of water and alcohol (50-50) will dry faster and help prevent warps. Do not force dry your wet model with a hair dryer or oven. This is a good way to put in warps. A slow air dry at room temperature will do it. I know several modelers who work on three or four projects at once just for something to

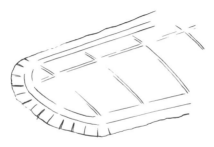

Fig. 7-6. Slit tissue to fold over at curved areas.

do while these wet parts are drying. This is a good time to work on your nose block prop or scale accessories.

This is the place where you *must* have a fixture to hold parts when drying. For a polyhedral wing spray the top and bottom of the center and the tip section (half the wing) then pin the center section flat with the tip blocked up at the proper angle. When dry, repeat with the other half. This allows top and bottom to dry at the same rate, again helping to prevent warps.

If your tissue is not dry and tight after the first water spray, try a bit more water in the local area. If this doesn't work, try losening the tissue with a bit of thinner and restretching. The above is much easier to do with the dope method rather than the white glue method.

Remember when we talked about "washout" in the wing construction section? In order to maintain the "washout" your dihedral fixture should still have the small shim at the rear of the wing. Therefore, when you

63

place the wet wing into the fixture the tissue shrinkage will help shape the correct angle. Please don't think this is one of those steps that is only for the expert or purist. Throughout this book I will constantly harp on warps and the damage they can do. Your model will fly much better with lots of wrinkled, sagging tissue and braces glued to the outside of broken spars than it will with just a few small warps in the right places. A left wing leading edge warped down 1/16″ or the same amount up on a right leading edge can result in a left spiral dive that will destroy your model before it ever gets to fly.

Now a word about patching since lots of tears occur right at the work bench. With large tears, it's easier to replace a whole section. Just cut out the tissue between sticks or ribs that surround the tear, dope the edges of the sticks, cut a patch just 3/32″ larger and stretch it over the edge sticks adhering with thinner as before. This will work even if you used the white glue method originally. I prefer this to trying to pull edges of a cut together and gluing them. Tissue seems to shrink up just a bit so the torn edges never quite meet. For field repairs, a patch can be doped right over a hole then a neater job can be done at home.

If you have particularly unsightly and stubborn wrinkled areas then you will have to remove the tissue and try to re-cover in smaller strips. This happens a lot around wingtip areas.

Now check for warps again. Wings can be checked by putting them across an open desk drawer (Fig. 7-7). The rear of each tip should be up slightly. Stab and rudder should lay flat on a glass surface. Eyeball your fuselage and make sure the dreaded "Banana" shape has not appeared. If you find a warp, steam it out before doping. Heat some water or run the shower red hot and let the bad part soak up some steam while twisting the warp out. *HOLD* the twist until the part cools or pin it into a fixture while still hot and damp. Repeat until the warp is gone.

Doping is next and a good job can improve both appearance and flyability. I use Nitrate dope mixed 50-50 with thinner. If Nitrate is hard for you to get, then Butyrate is OK with a few drops of Sig Retarder or Castor Oil to plasticize and slow shrinkage. The beginner will probably

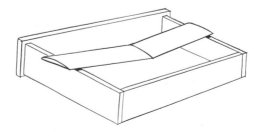

Fig. 7-7. Check wing for warps using open drawer.

buy dope in a 4 oz. bottle or smaller. Remember, this stuff is highly flammable and toxic so avoid spills and *ALWAYS* use it in a well ventilated area.

Many modelers build in the basement. This can be the worst place for doping, particularly if you are alone. Most of my friends set up in the garage to dope or work with wide open windows even if it gets cold. Dope vapor can collect in a closed room and suddenly knock you over.

On most tissue covered rubber models, two coats of 50-50 dope will do the job. This depends a bit on the type of tissue used and the coverage. Real Old Time tissue, as sold by Old Timer Models, has a shiny and a dull side. The shiny side absorbs less dope and may take an extra coat to get the finish you want. Champion tissue is very slightly heavier than Old Timer but absorbs dope more easily and gives you a harder gloss finish. Here the reader will have to experiment. An extra coat on the fuselage won't hurt but more than three coats and you are wasting weight.

I do not recommend spray cans because the dope is not thinned enough and you tend to overspray. I have been quite successful with the inexpensive foam rubber brushes sold in hardware stores. They spread dope beautifully and can be thrown away after one or two uses when they begin to shed.

Another interesting method for doping large areas is to lay a couple of sheets of toilet tissue over the area. Flood that tissue with dope by brush then drag it slowly over your covering tissue. The builder will simply have to experiment here to find the most comfortable and best looking method. Of course, air gun spraying is the best method but it requires more equipment and better ventilation. It is the only method capable of producing a light enough colored coating on scale models.

For larger models (36" and up) and the fuselages on 30" models, I use Silkspan. This is a fiborus tissue that can be dyed easily and applied damp to get the very best wrinkle free covering. Silkspan is considerably stronger than tissue and a bit heavier. It has a definite grain and looks almost like cloth. Sig sells a white 00 Silkspan that dyes easily with Rit which is available in a profusion of colors. Just soak the Silkspan in Rit and water as instructed, press excess water out between towels or rags, hang up to dry overnight and iron smooth. You can dye a dozen sheets in a sink in about 20 minutes and produce a pretty close match with another batch.

To apply, wet the Silkspan again and press out until only damp. Now you can apply using the dope method and the material will stretch around curves. You should be able to pull all the wrinkles out before shrinking. Be sure to mount in a fixture immediately to dry each side as applied. Doping is the same as tissue.

Color trim and decals can be applied right over the doped tissue. Tissue strips can be held in place with a drop of thinner and then adhered completely with thinner brushed right on. For sport models, windshields can be easily simulated with black tissue instead of transparent plastic. This makes for less work and a neater covering job. Clear windshields are described in the scale chapter.

After your model is doped and dry and you have admired it for a while and taken a picture or two, it's time to glue in the various hooks and locating keys that will keep it flying. Locate exactly where you want your keys, slit just through the tissue so you can glue wood to wood and tack them in. Assemble the model again to make sure the keys are right then take it apart and Cyano glue the keys in. Keys and hooks should always be glued to balsa or hardwood under the tissue. In "Construction" I suggested planning this before covering since many kits don't show it. At this point, please check again for warps. They can still be taken out by steaming as described before except that you will have to steam a bit longer. Also, dope may sometimes "Blush". This is a whitening of the surface and is caused by dampness. A quick coat of thinner then another thin coat of dope will handle that.

Now is the time to put your name and address on the model, in a location that will be easily noticed. I make up small labels that mention a reward to the finder and carry my phone number. So far, in ten years, I have lost eight models and had six returned. Even Pete Rose never batted that high.

If you want to do some covering without building a whole new model, convert the Courier to stick and tissue. Round off the top of the rib, take away the extra 1/8″ on the bottom and add a 1/16″ x 1/8″ spar at the highest point. Install a 3/32″ sq LE and a 1/16″ x 3/16″ TE. Ribs of medium 1/16″ spaced 1½″ apart will be fine. The tail should be 1/16″ sq with a few gussets. Cover with care, assemble as before and fly at 2/3 the previous weight.

Getting tissue off when required can be harder than putting it on. When white glue and water is used, be extremely careful when using water to soften the bond. Too much water will weaken and warp your structure. If dope and thinner was used, a slow application of thinner in small areas will work. Also, Red Devil #99 paint remover does a swell job if used sparingly and with care.

8

Propellers And Nose Blocks

This is probably the most neglected area in modeling. I admit that plastic props have allowed many modelers to participate without having to learn to carve but at the same time they restrict the modeler to only what they can do. The right prop can dramatically improve your model's endurance and smooth out the flight pattern. The right prop mounting will make all of your adjustments easier and reduce crash damage to a minimum, so let's start with noseblocks and hangers.

In the Canary and the Courier we used standard plastic prop hangers but we can do better with only a bit of work. The plastic hangers can't be adjusted for thrust and they tend to wear loose after a few flights. Of the three hangers in Fig. 8-1, the wire spring type is best for the beginner. Just lock a 1/8" drill or dowel in a vise, wind .030" wire three tight turns around it then bend as shown. This easily admits a 1/8" bushing so props can be changed in moments and thrust line adjusted by bending the wire.

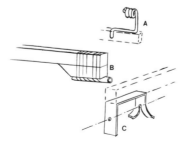

Fig. 8-1. Three different prop hangers A,B,C.

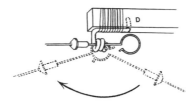

Fig. 8-1D. How hook slips into hanger A.

Method "C" is made by flattening a 1" piece of 3/32" aluminum tubing, drilling two holes 1/32" diameter, slitting one end to the hole and slightly separating it, then bending up both ends. This allows for a 1/32" wire hook without a bearing and is a bit lighter for indoor models or profile scale.

On full fuselage models where nose blocks are used, a little care in construction can save a lot of grief later on. Nose blocks should be made up of several layers of balsa with a plywood base sheet to mate with the nose of the fuselage. If practical, the grain should run parallel to the thrustline so the block won't crush as easily. Here a good drilling job is really important. If you don't have a drill press, try the local school shop. The bearing hole must be drilled as centered and as vertical as possible because it controls the thrust of the prop and, therefore, the direction of flight of your model. After drilling, I cut a slot like a keyhole above or below the bearing hole as shown. This allows me to slip a new prop with hook and bearing right in (Fig. 8-2).

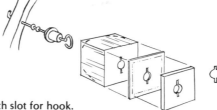

Fig. 8-2. Nose block with slot for hook.

At this point, I also rub in a coat of Cyano glue inside the bearing hole and around the edges of the block. This hardens the wood against later wear. On larger models (Coupe, Unlimited, Jumbo Scale, etc.) I create a split nose block held together by 2-56 nylon screws and using a brass bushing. I simply drill a clearance hole for the screw in one side of the block, then tap the other side and harden with Cyano. This allows me to insert different props while testing the model. The split block shown in Fig. 8-3 is then carved to shape.

The 2-56 nylon thrust adjusting screws mentioned in the construction chapter bear against the ply base of the nose block and push it out

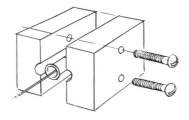

Fig. 8-3. Split nose block with brass bushing.

against the holding pressure of the rubber retainer band to adjust thrust (Fig. 6-10).

Propellers

There has been a great deal written about propeller pitch and pitch/diameter ratio. Much of it is filled with formulas and numbers that turn the beginner off. Pitch, diameter, blade area and airfoil certainly are very important but I believe the beginner and novice can learn to work with these factors without having to wade through a lot of math. Accordingly, I have made some assumptions that aren't strictly true but will serve to provide good approximations for practical construction.

The propeller is the gadget on the front (possibly on the rear) of your model that pulls it through the air and causes the wings to generate lift. Its rotation speed affects the speed of your model and the longer it runs the longer you will stay aloft. This is your first trade-off. If the prop runs faster, you climb higher. If it runs slower, it runs longer assuming the same rubber motor with the same winds. Therefore, for *each individual* model we have to try to find the prop/rubber/winds combination that will get us as high as possible and keep us up there the longest.

To do the above, we need to know a little about what makes props work. Look at your plastic prop from the tip of the blade towards the hub. You will see that it looks kind of like the thread on a screw. The British call the prop an "Airscrew" (Fig. 8-4). the "tilt" of that thread is the angle of the

Fig. 8-4. Side view of prop showing hub & tip angles.

screw which is called the "Pitch." If we assume that air has density (which it does) then the larger the pitch angle (the higher the pitch), the harder it will be for the prop to cut through and pull the plane along.

The higher the pitch the slower the prop will rotate, the slower the plane will fly and the longer the motor will run. This is great up to the point where the propeller doesn't turn fast enough and the plane falls out of the air. Now if we add that increasing blade area and prop diameter will have a similar effect to increasing pitch the problem seems very complicated. Let's make it even tougher. If you lengthen the rubber motor or reduce the size of the strands, you also slow the prop. If you haven't given up yet, the cavalry is just over the next rise.

Choosing The Right Prop

All of the above is true but experience has shown us that there is a range that is practical for most models and that if we start with a prop/rubber combination in that range we will probably have a flyable model. Later, experiments with small changes can "Fine Tune" your model for best performance. If the above hasn't scared you off, let's learn how to find the prop we want, then how to make it. Later we'll come back and learn the mathematics of pitch calculation and its relation to actual prop shape and angles.

As a first approximation, Table 8-1 shows the basic prop factors for three general types of models. These are based on wing area which is a more accurate method than one based on wing span. Wing area calculations were covered earlier. Another method that is quite accurate is to draw the wing to scale on graph paper, count the number of squares covered (estimate partial squares) and multiply by the appropriate scale factor. Don't forget to figure the area of *BOTH* wings.

Table 8-1 also introduces us to a new factor called "Pitch/Diameter Ratio" or "P/D" for short. P/D was invented to take some of the complication out of prop calculations. Since there is a direct relationship between pitch and performance and diameter and performance, it seemed reasonable that the ratio between the two (ratio is any one factor divided by the other as in Pitch divided by Diameter, etc. P/D) might be better then calculating each factor individually.

Let's take the Condor and see how we can design a prop. The wing is a rectangle 24" x 3" so the area is 72 sq in. The square root of 72 is 8:485. Square root can easily be found on most calculators or by approximation. A square root is the number which when multiplied by itself equals your target. For instance, 8 x 8 = 64 while 9 x 9 = 81 so the square root of 72 must be in between. For a sport model we want 1.1 x the square root of the wing area so our prop diameter is 1.1 x 8.5" = 9.32". Let's use 9". Pitch diameter ratio is given as 1.3 so pitch is 1.3 x 9" = 11.7". It is interesting to note that later on in the "Design" chapter we have a sketch that suggests that prop diameter should be .4 x Span. On the Condor that would be .4 x 24" = 9.16".

This all means that for a starting design for the Condor we should have a 9" diameter prop with a pitch of 11.7" and a maximum blade chord (the widest point on the blade) of 12% of the diamter of 1.08". The plan for the Condor calls for an 8" plastic prop because this will provide a more flyable model for the builder at that stage in his development. Generally, a smaller diameter, lower pitch prop will prove more flyable since it will fly the model a bit faster and keep it from the edge of a stall. After reading this chapter, try a larger prop on the Condor and re-trim for longer flights.

Now that we know what prop we need, the problem becomes how to get there. At this point I must split this narrative into one for the "How To" and one for the "Where-From" guys. For "How-To", I will show several methods for making prop blades and describe a way to mount the blades at a specific pitch angle. This will allow anyone to calculate prop factors as above, then use them to create the desired prop. Later, I will explain what pitch is and how to calculate it to make pitch blocks and props for all requirements.

Probably the easiest way to make prop blades is to cut them from an appropriate plastic cylinder. For blades up to 6-7", various containers like yogurt and cottage cheese work well. For the larger props up to 9-10", I cut them from the sides of 2 liter soda bottles. These are usually Lexan which is extremely tough and can be colored with Magic Markers. As long as the container has a 4-8" diameter it will work out.

First, draw a line at 15 degrees left of vertical on the bottle. Then lay out your blade outline with this line as the center. This is for a right hand tractor prop. Right hand means that the prop will rotate clockwise *AS SEEN BY THE PILOT*. For left hand props (usually seen on pusher models), slant the 15 degree line to the right. Simply cut the blade shape out of the bottle, slit a dowel with a razor saw and epoxy in the blade. I usually insure this joint by drilling two holes, 1/32" diameter, through the dowel and the blade and pushing in a piece of broom straw or toothpick (Fig.s 8-5 and 8-6).

I suggest that a separate piece of dowel be used for each blade. Then the

Fig. 8-5. Prop blade molded on bottle.

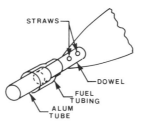

Fig. 8-6. Adjustable pitch free wheeler.

dowels can be put in an aluminum tubing hub at the correct angle for the pitch you want.

Mark Fineman has developed a similar method for blades from card stock. He glues two sheets of card stock together with white glue, tapes them to the outside of a 12″ stock pot and lets them dry overnight. He then marks his angle and blade shape, cuts out the blades and mounts them on a hub.

For larger blades, 10″ and up, I use balsa laminations. The plastic blades flex too much in the larger sizes. Using a piece of plastic pipe about 8″ diameter, I iron on two layers of balsa with dry white glue in between as described in the section on rolled fuselages. I have also made blades with two layers of balsa with Tyvec in between and they were extremely strong. I also cover all large balsa prop blades with silk. Sig carries it in several colors and, in a pinch, an old pair of panty hose will do. Apply the silk damp, as with silkspan, however, don't try to fold it over the edges. After the silk has been applied with thinner and dried, dope the ½″ or so of extra silk that sticks out over the edge. This becomes stiff when it dries and can be trimmed very close with a razor. Two or three coats of dope on top and your blades will withstand crackups that destroy the rest of the fuselage.

Setting The Pitch Angle

Now that we have a few ways of making blades and can attach them to dowel spars, we are ready to mount the blades in a hub at the pitch angle we require. Take one of your plastic props, turn it edge on, as in Fig. 8-4, and study it for a moment. You will notice that the blade is almost parallel to the thrustline at the hub and twists gradually so it is at an angle of 60 degress or more to the thrustline at the tip. Somewhere between the two points it must, therefore, pass through 45 degrees. If we can find the spot along the blade where it passes through 45 degrees we can find the pitch.

I'll show the formulas later but it must be obvious that if we can find the pitch at the 45 degree point, we can set any pitch we want by setting our blade in the hub so that it rests at 45 degrees at a particular spot along its slightly twisted length. Remember, the twist came in when we cut or formed the blade at a 15 degree angle on the cylinder.

All we need to accomplish the above is a movable 45 degree angle, a clamp or base for the prop hub and a special scale that reads in pitch as we move the angle out from the center. Fig. 8-7 shows a 14″ prop on the pitch gage with the 45 degree marker at about 18″ pitch. Note that the pitch gage can be used with a bare prop or one already mounted in a nose block. A diameter of 14″ and a pitch of 18″ corresponds to a P/D Ratio of 1.3 as described in Table 8-1, (1.3 x 14″ = 18.2″).

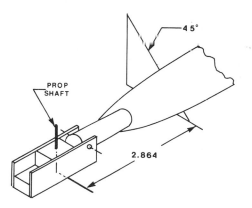

Fig. 8-7. Prop on gage set for 18″ pitch.

Table 8-1. Basic Propeller Design Factors.

ITEM	SCALE	SPORT	ENDURANCE
PROP DIAMETER	.8 $\sqrt{\text{(W.A.)}}$	1.1$\sqrt{\text{(W.A.)}}$	1.4$\sqrt{\text{(W.A.)}}$
MAX. CHORD	15%	12%	9%
P/D	1.4	1.3	1.2
SPAN	13-18″	18-36″	ABOVE 36″
BLADE THICKNESS	1/16″	3/32″	1/8″
From *Flying Models* Magazine 8/83			

Table 8-2 shows the scales you will need to set pitch. I have shown both 30 and 45 degree scales because it is best to set pitch somewhere between 25% and 75% of the prop radius and some props won't read well using 45 degrees.

Explanation Of Pitch

The "How-To" above will get anyone started on making his own props and provide a little understanding of the process. Props made this way are not truly helical and therefore, are less efficient. For those who want to go a step further the reward is not only a more efficient prop but also a

Table 8-2. Propeller Pitch Gage Settings

Pitch	8"	10"	12"	14"	16"	18"	20"	22"	24"	26"	28"	30"
45°	1.27	1.59	1.91	2.23	2.55	2.87	3.18	3.50	3.82	4.14	4.46	4.77
30°	2.21	2.75	3.30	3.86	4.40	4.96	5.51	6.06	6.61	7.16	7.71	8.26

Distances given are in inches from prop hub center to 45 or 30 degree point on blade, whichever occurs closest to midblade. To calculate 45° distance for any pitch, divide pitch by 2 pi. To calculate pitch from 45° radius, multiply radius by 2 pi. To calculate 30° distance, multiply pitch by 1.73 then divide result by 2 pi. To calculate pitch from 30° radius, multiply radius by 2 pi, then divide result by 1.73.

Note: This prop pitch chart and a lot more technical information can be found in William F. McCombs fine book, *Making Scale Model Airplanes Fly*.

system that can produce any number of correct pitch props from just a few carved forms.

Fig. 8-8 shows the path of the tip of one blade. The reciprocal path of the other blade has been omitted for clarity. This path is the helix we have been talking about and it covers the surface of a cylinder whose diameter equals the prop diameter and whose length is the *PITCH* of that particular prop. For example, the 14" prop in 8-7 with 18" pitch would describe a cylinder 14" in diameter and 18" long.

Study the above carefully. Once you understand it, all the rest is easy. Next, we'll take that cylinder, cut it along the helix line (it will look like the spiral wrapped cardboard tubes you find inside a paper towel or toilet

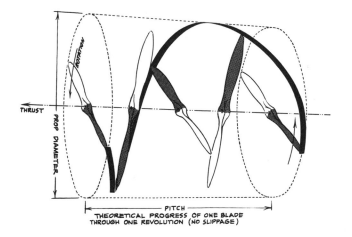

Fig. 8-8. Path of prop showing pitch length and helix.

74

tissue roll), and unroll it flat.

Fortunately it forms a right triangle and with some simple geometry we can do a lot with right triangles. B-C in Fig. 8-9 is our 18″ length; A-B becomes the circumference of a 14″ diameter which is Pi x D or 3.14 x 14″ = 43.979″. The angle at point A (angle BAC) can be calculated from a Tangent table or checked against a protractor as 22 degrees.

This is the tip angle of a prop with that pitch at that diameter. The pitch table in the Appendix will do all these calculations for you.

Look again at Fig. 8-9. Note the 45 degree point. At 45 degrees both sides of a right triangle (B-D and B-C) are equal. Since we know the blade starts at a very high angle, more than 60 degrees, near the hub (Fig. 8-4), and reaches 22 degrees at the tip, it passes through 45 somewhere along the radius. Now we can see from the diagram (Fig. 8-9) that the 45 point along the CIRCUMFERENCE LINE is at a distance equal to the PITCH!

To convert this important piece of information to practical use we follow the analysis only one more step. That 45 degree point defines the circumference of a mythical prop whose diameter would be the circumference length at that point (equal to the pitch length, 18″) divided by Pi (3.1414) because diameter = C/Pi. This would be 18″ divided by 3.1414 = 5.73″. Half of that, 5.73″/2 = 2.87″. This is the distance from the hub center to the 45 degree triangle on our Pitch gage (Fig. 8-7).

To get the distance on the Pitch gage just divide the pitch by 2 x Pi.

Prop Forming Block

Starting from the desired pitch and diameter we can now progress to the tip angle and then the dimensions of a block on which we can form

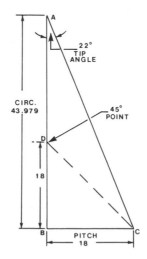

Fig. 8-9. Unrolled pitch cylinder.

75

accurate prop blades. The mathematics behind the tables and formulas is common practice in prop design. It is explained and illustrated most comprehensively in Ron Williams' book, "Building and Flying Indoor Models,, and, with Ron's permission, partially reproduced herein.

This concept is very important. It can save you hundreds of hours of future work and provide you with a re-usable library of Propeller Forming Blocks. A Prop Forming Block is a rectangular block of hard balsa or pine that has been carved with the flat shape of one side of one blade, thus requiring about 1/4 the time to carve a full prop. As Fig. 8-10 shows, soak a balsa blade of proper thickness and partially carved airfoil in water and ammonia and tape it to the form block with the blade center

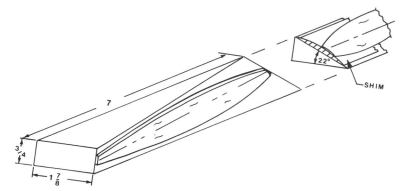

Fig. 8-10. Blade on prop form block.

aligned on the center of the block and the hub touching the vertical hub base of the block. The blade will now dry to the proper pitch.

The wonderful secret of the Prop Forming Block is that once you carve a specific pitch you can use that block for *any* diameter prop that requires the same pitch! In other words, if you carve a block for a 12″ diameter, 18″ pitch prop you can mold a blade for a 10″ diameter 18″ pitch prop on the same block.

With a bit of work on a winter weekend you can create a library of Forming Blocks that you can use for years to come. Start all your blocks 9″ long so you can eventually mold props up to 18″. Fig. 8-11 shows how to

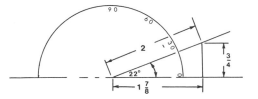

Fig. 8-11. Form block dimensions from tip angle layout.

76

calculate the height and width of the block for any tip angle. Rather than get involved with geometry, just decide on the biggest blade width you might want for any specific pitch and lay out a block height and width to get that blade size at the tip. For example, a block for our 14″ diameter 18″ pitch prop would be figured as follows:

Appendix 1-1 for prop pitch is arranged to show prop *RADIUS* (equal to 1/2 the diameter) along the top. Read down the 7″ column to get Pitch. You are looking for the nearest number to 18″ which turns out to be 17.872″. Follow this to the left column which will show you an angle of 22 Degrees which is the angle at the tip of your particular blade. Now all you need to do is set up a 22 degree angle using a protractor and measure along the *DIAGONAL* to reach 1.26″ which is you maximum blade chord (9% of 14″ from Table 8-1). Since the block will be used for other props allow a generous overage for carving — use 2″. Drop a perpendicular to get the height and width of the block and choose the nearest available stock. In this case, I came out with a block 3/4″ high by 1⅞″ wide (Fig. 11-12).

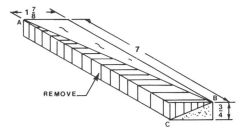

Fig. 8-12. How to carve a prop block.

If you can stand to read the above twice, you will have no trouble understanding how a prop or a form block is carved. Since plastic props do a pretty good job under 6″ diameter and a fair job from there to 9½″, I would start my form blocks at 10″ and go to 14″ for a start. If you do this, you can get away with only five form blocks at 12″, 15″, 18″ 21″ and 24″ pitch to cover most of the models you will build for a while.

The actual carving of the block is simple and instructive. Use a very sharp, thin bladed knife and remove material, using Fig. 8-12, from the area ABC. Check for flatness by holding the blade edge across the area. Sharpen your knife frequently and seal and dope the finished block with several coats. Remember that the hub point on your form block represents the center of the prop. If you are building a folder or mounting your blades in a hub, then make sure you move the blade out along the block until the outer tip of the blade conforms to the tip position on the block for that particular diameter. Also, if you want to mold undercamber into your blades, prepare a thin shim carved to the correct shape and lay it under the blade while molding, as shown cross hatched in Fig. 8-10.

It is important to round out this chapter with some discussion of carved props. It may seem a waste of time to consider carving a whole prop when you can mold blades so easily. Generally, this is true but as you progress into competition models the effects you can create with specially carved props become more critical. For instance, you can carve blades to have the same type of washout that you put into wings so they won't stall at the tips. True helical pitch is easy and transition points are smoother than with molded blades.

You can carve a prop by figuring the tip angle and carving each blade as if it were a form block. You can also lay out a block by deciding on your P/D ratio, diameter and maximum chord from Table 8-1, then refer to Figs. 8-13 and Table 8-3 as follows: From the previous example, our 14″

Table 8-3. Propeller Carving Factors.

Selected P/D	Block Width Factor Wb	Block Depth Factor Hb	Tip Depth Factor Ht
.9	.95	.45	.24
1.0	.94	.50	.27
1.1	.92	.54	.29
1.2	.91	.58	.31
1.3	.89	.62	.33
1.4	.88	.65	.35
1.5	.86	.68	.37
1.6	.85	.72	.39
1.7	.83	.75	.40
1.8	.82	.78	.42

From *Flying Models* Magazine 8/83

diameter, 18″ pitch prop has a maximum chord of 1.26″ and a P/D of 1.3 (18″/14″). From Table 8-3 we see that at P/D of 1.3 we have block *FACTORS* of Wb = .89, Hb = .62, Ht = .33. Now we can easily set up block dimensions by multiplying each factor by the maximum chord. Block width will be 1.26 x .89 = 1.12″; Height is 1.26″ x .62 = .78″ and depth at tip is 1.26″ x .33 = .416″. If we approximate to use standard stock then a block 14″ x 1⅛″ x ¾″ will do the job. Check Fig. 8-13 to see how these dimensions apply to prop shape.

Choose a block of fairly hard balsa with a smooth, even, straight grain, 8 lbs. density or more. Drill a center hole. Carve the rear face first, constantly checking for flatness with your blade edge. Carve the front to give an airfoil shape and the rear relief at the hub. Templates for blade thickness can be a big help in matching the blades to each other. Balance before adding free wheel or folding equipment.

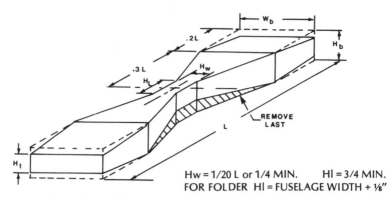

Hw = 1/20 L or 1/4 MIN.   Hl = 3/4 MIN.
FOR FOLDER Hl = FUSELAGE WIDTH + ⅛"

Fig. 0 13. Carved prop from Table 0 3.

For a long time, the only way to get a prop larger than the 9½" commercially available plastic ones was to carve or form your own as shown on the previous pages. Those modelers reluctant to try these techniques were restricted to smaller models with less performance. Finally, someone has appeared who is able to fill this very important supply gap. Now, without becoming an expert balsa chopper, you too can fly bigger models with more rubber and any size prop you choose.

Ed Wickland of Superior Props can supply any size or pitch prop, carved and ready for sanding. He has folder hubs, blades, a pitch gage and even a free wheeling hub with replaceable blades. Three or four blades, left and right hand pitch, are all available at very reasonable prices.

9

Freewheeling And Folding Props

Free Wheelers

By now, you can make props from a variety of materials and in any shape, diameter or pitch. As you progress from beginner's models through novice to advanced, this will become even more important since performance increases almost in direct ratio to the efficiency of your prop. This brings us to the next level in propeller technology. Your flight profile passes through three phases; climb, cruise and glide. The prop is working in only the first two. In the glide it is worse than excess baggage, it can produce tremendous drag and, if allowed to continue to rotate in the slipstream, it will wind the rubber backwards and impede flight.

Early modelers noticed this and devised the free wheeling propeller to try to solve the problem. Some designers feel that the free-wheeler does less good than a disk of plywood on the nose but I don't agree. Having lost several models with plastic free-wheelers, I'm sure they do a ton of good. Anyway, almost all free wheeling devices are based on the latch principle in which the prop shaft catches in the latch when driven by the rubber in one direction but slips by when the prop starts to rotate by itself. Of the ones shown, the ramp type is the simplest but, I find the "Z" latch the surest. The spring latch can also act as a rubber tensioner which helps to keep the rubber from completely unwinding and bunching inside to change your balance (Fig. 9-1).

Folders

For real performance, a folding prop is necessary. Not only will your model's performance increase significantly, the thrill you get when your first folder climbs your model to three hundred feet then closes with an

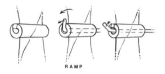

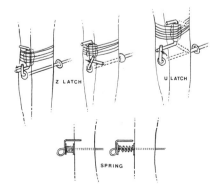

RAMP

Z LATCH   U LATCH

SPRING

Fig. 9-1. Four kinds of free wheelers.

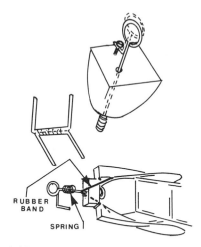

RUBBER
BAND

SPRING

Fig. 9-2. Carved prop with hinge.

audible snap is worth the extra effort. Also, your prop will fold on impact thus saving lots of repairs.

Basically, a folding prop is made just the same as any other then hinged along the hub to fold back against the fuselage sides. Also, a folder must have some arrangement with the shaft hook so that it will stop in the proper position for blades to lay flat and even. This is usually a

81

spring that extends when the rubber slackens, pulling the hook forward so it contacts a screw in the rear of the nose block. This is much less complicated than it sounds. Fig. 9-2 describes it better.

The RN Models folding set-up is about the simplest to build. Make your blades as before. Drill tubing for the hinge pin then simply push it on to the blade. It will cut its own slits. Set up your pitch by putting a wire through the hinge pin hole in the tubing *BUT* remember that the pin is to be HORIZONTAL in your pitch fixture not vertical as on all the other props, and epoxy the blade to the tubing. Then just build your hub and pin in the blades. With these systems you can easily replace blades by using wheel retainers to keep the hinge pins in (Fig. 9-3).

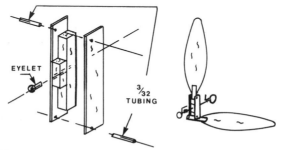

Fig. 9-3. RN folder.

The "Z" hub is used in most competition models and is quite a bit more complex and requires careful soldering but, it is the lightest and most efficient. Fig. 9-4 shows one type.

Note that the "Z"-bar is bent at a rather complex angle This allows the blades to fold flat against the fuselage sides thus reducing drag. This angle is between 7 and 11 degrees for most props and can be cut into the prop block, drilled in an RN-type system or bent into a "Z"-bar. More

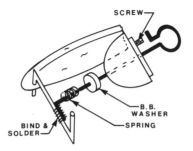

Fig. 9-4. " Z" hub folder.

sophisticated contest plans describe this in detail.

Do not assume that the air stream will hold your prop in the folded position. Fig 9-2 shows a small rubber band (solid line) that runs from the prop blade to the hub. This folds the blade and holds it. Mount the prop, place the bands and make sure they tend to pull against the extended blades. The spinning force of the prop under power will easily keep the blades open.

Adjustable Pitch

Two other ideas I have developed allow for the changing of pitch without re-building the prop. The first is designed for free wheelers where the blade is glued to a ¼" dowel that is slipped inside ¼" ID aluminum tubing for a hub. Simply slide ¼" fuel tubing over both. The tubing is tight enough to hold pitch adjustment during flight but can be forced into new adjustment by twisting hard (Fig. 8-6).

Fig 9-5 shows another idea that can be developed from a modification of the RN folder. Use eyelets to pivot the hub tube so it is clear through the center. Epoxy a steel 2-56 nut and a ¾" long piece of ¼" OD rubber tubing to the blade. Now insert a 2-56 steel screw through the tubing and into the nut. The assembly can now be slipped into the ¼" ID aluminum tube pivoted in the hub. As the screw is tightened, the rubber will bulge inside the tube and hold the blade in the desired position.

As you get more sophisticated in building and start to use folding props, some extra care is necessary to make sure the shaft is centered very accurately and the blades are balanced and true. You are now dealing with considerably more mass rotating at a pretty good clip so problems that were minor before begin to get serious very fast.

Balancing is required with any prop and we can cover that quickly

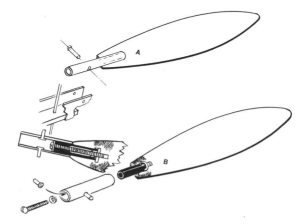

Fig. 9-5. RN folder modified for adjustable pitch.

here. With plastic props, just mount on a straight shaft, lock the shaft in a vise horizontally then add epoxy to the light blade or scrape the heavy blade until the prop will rest in any position. For competition P-30 props, you are not allowed to scrape the blades so, adding weight is your only method.

Balance all other props, carved or molded, as described above but now also make sure the blades are equal in area, shape, airfoil and pitch. Before, you were working on "Static" balance which is only making sure the prop is balanced at rest. Now we have to get into "Dynamic" balance which is making sure the prop rotates in balance. All the factors mentioned above affect dynamic balance, and pitch is the most important. Earlier I described a simple pitch gage to set each blade. For those who skipped this, you are no longer a beginner and the effect of unequal pitch can cut your performance by 30 - 40%! The vibrations set up can actually throw your model into a death spiral during the climb phase.

The cure is simple and starts before you carve the first blade. Be careful to choose a sheet or block that is equal in weight and hardness, then match and weigh the blades after carving. Prop blade sets sold by Champion Models are sawn to basic shape and matched for hardness *and* weight. Last, create the kind of fixture that will help match the pitch of the blades. Now you can also see that the noseblock is a fairly important feature and must be as true as the prop. A worn noseblock should be replaced. On larger models, the split block with brass bushing for the prop is very useful and adds little weight.

10

Rubber

Rubber is the motor of your model and should be treated with vast respect. A small mistake with a wound motor and you can instantly "re-kit" your model. On the other hand, proper choice of rubber, good storage habits and good winding technique can vastly increase performance. I have models 10 and 12 years old that are still flying. The Beautiful Bess on the cover has had motors break several times with no damage and these were 12 strands of ¼" rubber x 36" long.

The very best rubber used to be made by the Pirelli Company of racing tire fame. I believe it was used to tie grape vines and, later, in golf balls. This rubber returned the most energy for its weight. Unfortunately, Pirelli has gone the way of the Buffalo. Quite good rubber is available from FAI, Champion, Sig, Peck and others. Although each batch differs somewhat, the table for winds will serve as a good guide.

Rubber is available in hanks weighing about a pound and in sizes of 1/16", 3/32", 1/8", 3/16" and 1/4". Smaller packages down to 25' are also available. Rubber strippers that can cut almost any width from larger strips run the gamut from $25 to over $100. Jim Jones makes a very good one that doesn't cost too much. For the beginner though, I recommend buying rubber in widths of 3/32", 1/8" and 3/16" for a start.

The best test results we have seem to show that rubber should be stored in the refrigerator. Keep cool and away from light and pack in airtight bags to slow the natural vulcanizing process.

Rubber can be left with the talcum on while stored but before use should be washed in cool water with mild soap to remove all the talc and other debris. Make up your motor by putting two nails in a board at the distance that defines each loop then simply wrap the rubber around the nails to get the number of strands you want. Always try to make up an

85

even number of strands so you can work with a simple knot. Your rubber must be wet when you tie your knot. This allows you to pull the knot very tight. Then wet some more and pull even tighter. Fig. 10-1 shows how to tie a knot and insure it with a drop of Cyano. Fig. 10-2 was shown in the February 1979 issue of *Model Builder* and is attributed to Dr. Edward Hunter. It is supposed to hold even a lubed rubber.

Some builders also tie a short piece of wool or put a drop of Cyano glue on the outer side of the knot to prevent slipping.

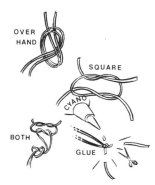

Fig. 10-1. Basic rubber knot.

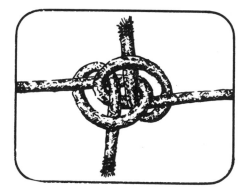

Fig. 10-2. Dr. Hunter's knot.

Choosing A Motor

This may be a good time to discuss how to choose a motor. As a rough approximation, your motor should weigh between 25 and 30% of the weight of the finished model *including* rubber. Some large competition models go as far as 40%. Its length should be about 1½ times the length

86

Fig. 10-3A. Pushing stick.

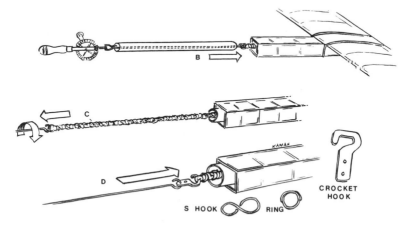

Fig. 10-3B,C,D. Winding Tube sequence.

from post to hook. If practical, the rubber should mount in the model so that when wound it extends 50% on either side of the CG. A very rearward hook as on old time models may not do much good at all. It tends to add weight to the rear which must be balanced by more weight and also adds lots of stress to the weakest portion of the model where it can twist the tail if it doesn't break it off. On Old Timer planes, I move the rear rubber hook at least one bay forward.

With the approximate motor weight decided, work out the best CROSS SECTION for your model. CROSS SECTION is the width of the rubber times the number of strands. For instance, a 15 gram motor can be 4 strands 3/16″ x 30″, or 6 strands 3/16″ x 20″, or 8 strands 1/8″ x 22½″. Power run time will be different on each. The thinner motor will run longer and smoother but with less peak power.

Next, break-in should NEVER be ignored. It takes less than 10 minutes and greatly extends motor life. If wound to 75% without break-in, a motor will get "tired" after 3 flights.

Breaking In the Rubber

Here's all you need for a good break-in. Stretch your motor to three times its rest length and hold for two minutes. While stretched, work some lube into the rubber with your fingers. Allow to rest for 10-15 minutes then stretch again to 4-5 times rest length and hold for 4 minutes. That's all you need to do. The lube referred to is available through most sources like Sig and Peck or you can make your own using glycerin and green soap from the local drugstore. If you do, however, you must simmer the green soap to remove the alcohol since the drugstore stuff is really "tincture" of green soap which is mixed with alcohol. K-Y jelly is also a fair lube but it doesn't last too long on the rubber. I am experimenting with some new silicone greases but I don't know yet if they will cause deterioration. Do not use vaseline or any other petroleum grease. It will destroy your rubber. Just enough lube to make the rubber slippery is the rule. Too much and it will splash all over the fuselage weakening your glue joints and spotting the tissue. Keep your lube in a 1 oz. plastic bottle with a squeeze spout. Dispense a few drops into a plastic baggie, drop in your motor and rub the mixture together. Also, you can try the photographer's film squeegee. Just attach small pads of sponge rubber to the ends of each side of a standard film squeegee, put a few drops of lube on the pads and run the rubber between them.

Winding Tube

Once lubed and made up, insert your motor in the model by following the steps in Fig. 10-3.

Mount the motor on a pushing stick (A), so you can slide it down inside the fuselage and catch it with the rear tube or peg. Marty Taft makes interesting pushing sticks by building a forked end and gluing it to the end of one of those teacher's extendible pointers that comes with a pocket clip. This works very well for small models.

Now take a long wire hook (at least the length of the fuselage), slide it inside your winding tube and hook it to your winder on one end and your "S"-or Crocket hook (attached to the rubber) on the other. Pull the rubber out of the fuselage into winding position and slide the winding tube inside the fuselage. The winding tube should be a smooth slide fit in the nose opening and should go all the way to the rear peg. Some builders slot the rear end of the winding tube so it slides over the rear motor peg to give absolute protection. Now you can go through the winding procedure until the Crocket hook reaches the nose block. Then slide the tube out along the wire hook. *BEFORE* removing the wire hook, slip a piece of 1/16" wire through your "S"-hook at the nose to hold the rubber firmly while you remove the winder and the wire hook and attach your prop. This way you will have control of the wound rubber at all times. Believe me, the first time you break a big, wound motor inside a winding tube *WITH NO*

DAMAGE you will be glad you took the time to learn this. Besides, in a contest you will have to go for maximum power to win and without a winding tube this will be a very stressful procedure. Winding tubes can be any strong material from high tech plastic to carboard. A plug of soft foam rubber pushed into the nose around the tube will keep it in place. Some builders even make a disk of plywood that fits the front of the tube and protects the nose in case of motor rupture.

Before discussing the actual techniques of winding, let's look over the tools you might be using. The pushing stick and wire hook should be filed free of burrs and nicks and padded with fuel tubing where they contact the rubber. The motor should be newly lubed and examined for nicks, holes and foreign matter before installation. Since your rear rubber anchor is aluminum tubing, it's easy to hold the model securely in a stooge by running a piece of heavy wire through the tube. My stooge attaches to my car door but most are ground mounted as in Fig. 10-4.

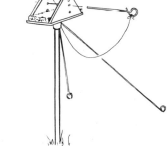

Fig. 10-4. Winding stooge.

Winders

Winders made from drills can be dangerous if you simply clamp the hook in the chuck. The winding torque will eventually slip the hook loose and since this will occur at maximum pull, the results can be disastrous to the model and injurious to the modeler. (I try always to wind with a stooge rather than a helper. This gives me more control over the model and much less chance for injury.) To make a winder from a drill, remove the chuck, drill a hole through the main shaft and bend and solder a wire hook as in Fig. 10-5. Peck and others sell small 5:1 or 6:1 winders that are OK to about four strands of 3/32" but mostly good for one loop motors. "Scalewinder" sold by Rees Industries or the full sized winder made by

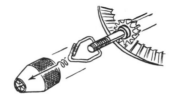

Fig. 10-5. Drill modified as winder.

John Morrill are also very good products. Scalewinder has a 10:1 ratio which makes it perfect for those 10-15 gram motors used in most scale models.

Most beginning modelers don't seem to pay much attention to the size and shape of the hook they use to attach the prop to the rubber. I think this is a big mistake. An off center hook will add a lot of vibration to your power run and cost you climb and duration besides lots of wear on the nose. A hook that is too small or the wrong shape might allow the rubber to "climb" the hook and jump right off while fully wound. My UK friend, Jeff Anderson, totally destroyed a 55" span unlimited model this way. The only thing he had left when the smoke cleared was the terrific color picture his son snapped at the critical instant.

I use Crocket hooks on all my models. The rubber is looped over the hook and held tight to it with a small rubber band. For small models, Fig. 10-6 shows a hook that can be bent to prevent rubber climbing. Follow

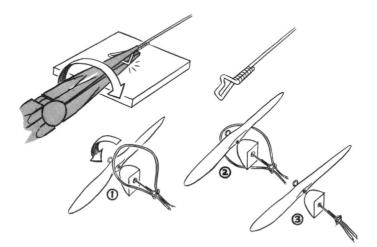

Fig. 10-6. Special hook to eliminate climbing rubber.

90

steps 1,2,3 to connect hook and rubber.

If you now have a winder, a stooge, various winding tubes, lube and pushing sticks, you are ready to wind. Right here I would suggest winding a couple of motors to destruction *outside* the model so you can get an idea of torque and pull.

Winding

Table 10-1 shows the maximum number of winds you can get from an *average* rubber motor of a certain size and number of strands. This is interesting to study for a moment. Note that it appears as if 8 strands of 1/8" rubber can be wound to the same number of turns per inch as 4 strands of 1/4" (48.7), but this is not really so. It is a close approximation. You can probably get 5 8% more winds in an equal weight of smaller rubber.

Table 10-1. Maximum Turns Per Inch For Rubber Motors.

Strands	Rubber Width		
	1/8"	3/16"	1/4"
2	97	83	69
4	69	59	49
6	56	48	40
8	49	41	34
10	43	37	31
12	40	34	28
14	37	31	26
16	34	28	23

Notes: 1. Above values are approximate. Each batch of rubber should be tested before winding.
2. Do not wind more than 80% max. For sport flying.
3. Above values based on full break in and stretch winding.
4. Approx. rubber weight: 1/8" = 1 gm/ft
   3/16" = 1.5 gm/ft
   1/4" = 2 gm/ft

From *Flying Models* Magazine 1/84

Contest rubber motors are weighed rather than measured for size and length. This makes for a closer match in power of different models. For instance, P-30 calls for a motor of 10 grams while the weight of the model without rubber must be a minimum of 40 grams. On the other hand, Coupe d'Hiver calls for the same 10 gram motor but the model must weigh either 80 or 100 grams. Also, P-30 props are 9½" in diameter while Coupe props are 14-16" in diameter. Coupes usually take a standard P-30 motor and double the strands while halving the length to get a short burst of real power to spin that big prop. Yet both try for 2 minute maxes.

The above information is merely intended to show the tremendous differences in models that can be categorized by specifying the weight of

91

the rubber. Along with the wind table, I have shown some very approximate weight vs. length figures for different rubber sizes. This is intended only as a rough guide for sizing motors. For accurate trimming or contest work you will need a scale.

Good winding technique takes a bit of practice. After you are all set up with stooge and tube, stretch the rubber to 3 times its length. Start winding and hold your distance until 50% of the turns are in. By then you will wish you had listened to me and tried a couple of destruction winds because the rubber will feel on the edge of bursting. Put that 50% in slowly while massaging the rubber to avoid big knots and evenly distribute the smaller knots. Now start walking in *slowly* while increasing the winds to 80%. By that time you should have reached the nose block. Remove your winder and tube as described above and you are ready to launch.

With more experience, you can hold your first position until 60% of the winds are in, then add winds to 85-90% of total. Unless I really need it for a contest, I never go above 85-90% of total. Care with knot distribution will result in smoother flights and may avoid stalls in the cruise portion of your flight. I've covered winding before braiding, even though you should braid all motors longer than the fuselage before your first flight. Most beginners will tend to ignore braiding and be eager to fly so I wanted to show what a loose motor can do. By bunching at front or rear (usually rear because the fuselage is skinnier there and traps the rubber) your motor can easily upset the balance of the model and cause stalls or dives.

Braiding

Braiding, as shown, is simple and quick and allows you to use much longer motors. You can divide your motor into two equal halves if practical, (4, 8, 12, 16 strands) or with one side a bit larger. Just divide your strands in half, attach your "S"-or Crocket hook at the middle point

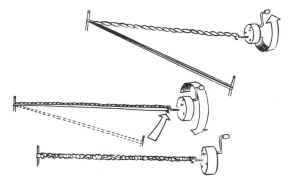

Fig. 10-7. Braiding a motor.

and hook it over a peg or nail. Now crank in 100-125 winds clockwise in one half of the motor. Hook the two ends together and wind backwards until the motor has smooth row of knots. Massage a bit with lube and you have a shortened motor that has lost only very little of its turn potential (Fig. 10-7).

Fig. 10-8 shows how to braid a single loop as might be used on a Peanut or Embryo. Just hold one end of the rubber in your mouth and roll some turns into it *BEFORE* tying the knot.

Braiding is not as essential if you have a spring tensioner on the prop shaft as on a folder. This will keep the rubber from becoming fully unwound.

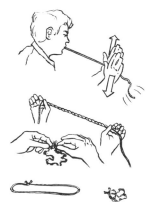

Fig. 10-8. Braiding a single loop.

Torque Meters

As you progress, you should begin to learn about torque meters. Torque is the twising force the rubber applies as it is wound. You feel this as a reverse twisting pressure on your hand and it gives some indication of how tight your motor is. A torque meter is a device that measures this force and this can be done right as you are winding. While some meters measure absolute torque in units of inch-ounces or inch-pounds, the most common is simply a wire which when twisted moves a pointer along a dial to register a number that can be used for comparison. By testing a motor of a certain size rubber with a certain number of strands, in say a 10 or a 12 inch length, the breaking torque *number* for that specific motor make-up can be determined. That number will then be close to the truth for *any* motor made up of the same size and number of strands *for any reasonable length*. In other words, if you test a motor 1/8″ x 4 strands x 12″ long and it breaks at number 6 on your meter, then another motor of 1/8″ x 4 strands and 30″ long will probably break at around number 6.

Fig. 10-9 shows a simple meter you can build. I believe this idea originated with Jim O'Reilly. The disk is epoxied to the brass tube and the tube is soldered to the wire at A. The pointer is soldered to the wire at B. When you wind, the rubber torque will twist the wire between A and B causing the pointer to rotate against the disk. If you fly many sizes of models you will need several meters since one size wire won't cover the whole range. Keep your length A-B at least 6" and choose wire sizes that twist between 45 and 180 degrees for each range: .015" wire for indoors, .030" for Peanut through 18", .045" up to 30" and .060" from there on. Make up a few test motors of each size, break them in and wind to destruction. Record the torque numbers as you go along so you will know the 60, 75, 80 and 90% points and use these in winding. Remember that each new batch of rubber will require testing. Torque winding is much safer and more accurate than counting turns and may just give you the edge you need to win.

As you can see from the foregoing, rubber is not the mystery you thought it was. With reasonable care and the correct equipment you can protect your models and fly them indefinitely.

Your rubber motors will also last a very long time if you wash and dry them after use, store away from light and air in a cold place, and re-lube before using. Also, try to keep your motor away from direct sunlight when at the field. Sunlight will affect your motor even through tissue. If you keep several models in your car at the field, cover them and leave the car windows open, as heat will also age rubber.

For sport flying or practice, try to stay around 75% of full power. This

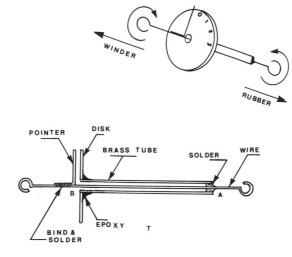

Fig. 10-9. Torque meter.

will help the rubber to last longer. For contests you should use a new, broken-in motor for each flight if practical.

Now, what do you do when you spot a nick or hole in a rubber strand as you start to wind? *STOP.* Unwind. One broken strand can cause a whole motor to blow up. A broken strand can be tied. Knot #2 shown at the beginning of this chapter will hold even practically lubed rubber although, I prefer to wash the rubber and retie.

Some builders, by careful application of Cyano glue, can even tie the broken strand while the rest of the motor is still made up and lubed. The ability to fix a broken strand is one reason why I prefer more strands of smaller rubber. For instance, two loops of 1/8″ rather than one loop of 1/4″.

When winding and when flying note that the torque or energy returned by the rubber is not constant. There is a burst of power that is often twice cruise power or more in the first seconds. When practicing with a torque meter, notice how the torque seems to increase suddenly as you approach 75 or 80% of full turns. Try moving in or out as you wind to see how this affects the torque readings. With a little practice you can get a lot more turns in than you were getting by counting. Also, some knowledge of how rubber acts will help you in trimming your model for contest flight.

A torque meter can also be used to tell you if the new rubber you just bought or took out of storage is average, better or worse than standard. Besides comparing the breaking torque number of new rubber with your previous records, recall the "pattern" of the torque vs. turns. For instance, at what percentage of full winds did the torque suddenly jump from number 4 to 5?

Good records of torque, flight times and patterns will help you a lot in trimming for consistent flight under all conditions. For those who are not ready for torque meters, a crude test for new rubber is to stretch a piece to 7 or 7½ times its rest length. If it becomes hard before reaching test length it is too brittle. If it stretches much beyond it is too soft.

11

Flight Trimming

This is the toughest chapter in the book. In past chapters I've said there are not absolutes. Here I have to tell you there aren't even any close approximations, just guiding principles that often depend on each other.

Even the best built model requires a careful flight trimming program. Remember that in a full scale or even an R/C model there is a pilot available to correct bad flight attitudes and to control the airplane through the various phases of flight. A FF (Free Flight) model must go through the three basic flight phases of climb, cruise and glide, with no guidance. In addition, a rubber powered model must climb smoothly through an irregular power output that may include a first burst that equals more than twice the torque of the rest of the motor run.

As if that weren't enough, we would like this model to recover from upsets caused by gusts, to turn into the wind, even in a glide, and to hunt for thermals so it can turn into one when found, and glide to win. Actually, all that can be done with careful adjustments made in small increments, one at a time, and without fancy gadgets to change the stab incidence or the rudder trim at different times in the flight. In 1987 Bob White won the coveted Wakefield Cup with a model that had only a folding prop and a D.T. No special gadgets at all. This was no fluke. Bob had been on the team many times before with the same type of model and come within seconds of winning. Also, this same basic model scaled to various sizes has won in P-30, Coupe and Unlimited.

In order to flight trim even the simplest model, we must learn a bit about flight technology but, I promise to adhere to the "KISS" Principle (Keep It Simple Stupid).

Wing Loading

Rather than discuss the various factors controlling flight as most texts do, we will start with "stability" as our first goal. Stability can be defined as "able to last" or "resistant to sudden change." Surely this is something we want for the model that we have spent all this time building. Once we get our model stable, we can concentrate on increasing performance.

An arrow is a very stable flying machine. Granted it doesn't have a lot of glide but, it generally goes where it is pointed and doesn't tumble or even rotate on the way. We can learn something from the arrow even if it isn't an airplane. An arrow is a well balanced object whose lines are true and straight. It has vanes on the rear that keep it straight in flight and, if you hold one, it has a practical "feel" to it. You feel as if you could throw it fairly straight because the balance feels natural. Also, an arrow has a minimum flight speed. At any lower speed, it will begin to fall and tumble. If we added proper wings to the arrow, we could increase the length and time of flight and decrease the minimum speed. In other words, we could begin to make it fly. As we increased the wing area on the arrow, we would reach some point that would allow it to glide, perhaps even to climb. Let's analyze your model the same way.

In order to fly instead of acting like a projectile (the arrow), our model must be light enough for its wings to carry it or we must increase the wing area. This exercise is known as checking the wing loading and is what really controls your flight profile. In most models, the wing is doing all the lifting. The prop and rubber provide the thrust, the tail group provides the control and the whole structure has weight and drag. It is the interaction between these four forces that affects flight.

If your model is too heavy (wing loading too high) it simply won't fly. Even if you add rubber to increase power and, therefore, speed you may not get much more than a powered glide to the ground. It's not possible to give you a hard and fast rule about weight but let's move from weight measured in grams or ounces to Wing Loading which is the weight per square inch or square foot of the wing. This is a better tool than weight alone.

First measure the area of your wing. Various methods for calculating wing area were discussed in Chapter 4.

A very good wing loading for small models is 0.33 grams per square inch. A Peanut with a 13″ span and a 2″ chord can fly at a weight of 13 grams but will do much better at 9 grams. For mid-sized models (24-30″ span), 0.5 gms./sq. in. is OK. A P-30 should weigh 50 grams minimum, including rubber, with a span of 30″. Although minimum chord is not specified in the rules, the average P-30 runs a 4″ chord. Therefore, with an area of 120 sq. in. (4″ x 30″) and a minimum weight of 50 grams with rubber, we have a wing loading of .416 (50/120) grams per square inch. This is less than our .5 base so we can expect a very good flying model.

Now most beginners build a little heavier, so a P-30 might be expected to come out closer to 60 grams than 50 thus hitting our .5 rule right on the button.

To weigh these models we need an accurate scale. A very good postal scale will do this but the cheaper ones just aren't accurate enough. Micro-Air Products sells a dandy sort of kit/plan for under $5.00 that can be built in an hour and is accurate to 0.1 grams (Fig. 11-1). If you work better in ounces and feet, with 28.35 grams per ounce and 144 sq. in. to a square foot, our 0.5 grams per sq. in. becomes:

$$0.5 \times 144 \, / \, 28.35 = 2.54 \text{ oz.} \, / \text{ sq. ft.}$$

Let's check that weight calculation against our three basic models. We'll weigh each one with and without rubber. Of course the weight with rubber is the real flying weight but the weight of the airframe becomes important in later design problems. Table 11-1 shows the comparisons.

As you can see, all the loadings are well under the 0.5 limit. This is one reason why all these models fly well. The AMA Racer which has the lowest wing loading is built of stick and tissue rather than all sheet and you can see how much weight has been saved. Certainly models that have a higher wing loading can fly. As your model grows larger, the wing loading can go up.

There is a basic rule in FF modeling that reads "Bigger Flies Better."

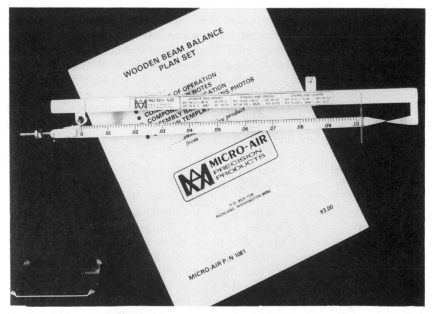

Fig. 11-1. Micro-air scale.

Table 11-1. Weight Breakdown And Wing Loading Of Various Models.

Model	Wt. (gms)	Rubber Wt	Total Wt	Wing Area	Wing Loading
Canary	8.0	2.0	10.0	24	.416
AMA Racer	8.0	2.0	10.0	36	.278
Courier	17.5	3.0	20.5	54	.379
Condor Wing	7.5				
Fuse	11.0				
Tail	3.5				
Prop	6.0				
L.G.	3.5				
Total	31.5	4.5	36	72	.500

Total weight in grams, wing area in sq. in. and wing loading in gms/sq. in.

This is true to a large degree and one of the reasons is that a larger model can fly with a higher wing loading. However, going much above that 0.5 is not recommended for the beginner since the model immediately becomes much faster and harder to trim. Try to keep your model around 0.45 or less at the start and you will do well.

Assuming you have followed previous chapters and built a model that is relatively warp free and clean lined and you have held the weight within limits, our next step is balance.

Balance

Note that weight was the first of the "trade-offs" I mentioned earlier. More weight, more speed, less duration. Balance will be the second trade-off. The closer to the nose your model balances, the more stable it will be. A heavily nose-weighted model will certainly go where you point it and will not be upset by gusts. Unfortunately, it won't fly very far either. For the beginner, your balance point should be somewhere between 25% and 40% of the wing chord from the Leading Edge. This will be called the CG, or Center of Gravity, of the model. I suggest that beginners start with a 25% CG. After you have trimmed the model for the rest of the flight profile you can gradually move the CG back 1/8" at a time to see if and how this improves the performance.

Trimming The Canary

In most built up and in almost all scale models, the wing is locked into one position fore and aft so CG changes must be made by adding weight. However, in our first three simple models we can shift the wing within wide limits for balance. These are good models on which to practice flight trimming because adjustments are simple and the structures are rugged. Their flight profiles however, are limited and some of the more subtle adjustments can only be made on more complex models like the Condor. Therefore, let's start with these first three, trim them for the best we can get, then use what we learned to move on to the Condor.

Note that on each plan (and in the chapter on improving the AMA Racer) a maximum nose length is given. Moving the wing any further back than this will result in a too short tail moment arm, (the distance that turning forces caused by the tail will act through), and will make turning and pitch recovery more difficult. Therefore balance each model on your fingertips 1/4 to 1/3 back from the LE. If the model is trail heavy, move the wing back. This is the same as adding nose weight. If it won't balance with the wing at maximum nose length position, add a small drop of clay to the nose. Most modelers absolutely dread adding weight to their creations. I guess they feel that this will-reduce duration. With a properly balanced model, though, your flight profile can vastly improve and add a lot to duration.

You are now ready for your first test glide. This should be over tall grass and in absolutely calm weather, if possible. I usually do glide tests in the early morning or evening when the wind seems to die down. Hold the model at shoulder height with the nose pointing very slightly down and aim at a spot on the ground about 20 feet in front of you. If there is any wind at all, face directly into it or a hair to the left. Now release the model with only a very slight push towards your aiming point. A few practice motions will teach this quickly. You are trying to get your model to glide forward about 20 feet as it descends 4 feet. This is only a five to one glide ratio and should be achieved by most models. If your model has been properly balanced, this first glide should work out OK. If the model dives steeply then check your balance and alignment again. On these models, the tail group (stab and rudder) is glued on so be sure they are level and true. A crooked tail group will destroy your flight profile. If the Canary is balanced and true and still dives, then slip another 1/32" shim under the wing LE. If it stalls (turns nose up and falls off backwards or to the side) then add a small drop of nose weight to bring the CG a bit forward.

We will allow the left turn for these three models to simplify trim procedures, however most high winged rubber powered FF models should turn right in the climb to avoid a Torque induced left spiral that can result in a crash. Since each of these models represents a distinct advancement in complexity from the one before, we will have to discuss their trim problems one at a time.

With a fairly good glide on the Canary, wind the rubber about 50-80 turns, hold the model in glide position and release with almost no push at all. The Canary should fly level or slightly descending and turn in a left circle about 30-40 feet in diameter. If the Canary flies straight or right and your alignment is still correct then bend the rudder tab a bit to the left. Keep these tab adjustments to only 1/32" at a time. This rudder adjustment acts the same as when you stick out your left foot behind a sled to make it turn left. The rudder tab acts in the slipstream to create additional drag on that side which causes the model to try to turn to the left around its CG. Rudder tabs should not be larger than 1/3" of the rudder and should not be turned more than 30 degrees to either side. If this is not enough then we can employ other techniques.

Once your gentle left turn is achieved, add power 50 turns at a time. You may find as you reach 150 turns or so that the Canary begins to tilt to the left very sharply as it turns and climbs. This is the Torque force beginning to act as the power of rubber increases.

On the Canary we can't tilt the nose bearing to counteract Torque so we use the small tab on the left wing TE. This tab acts as an aileron and produces a bit more lift on the left wing to help hold it up in a circle. Care must be taken with tabs, though. They can produce both lift and drag and that is another of our trade-offs. If the tab is too large or if it is turned too much into the slipstream, the drag it induces will counteract its lift. Each wing tab should not extend more than 1/2 to 3/4" beyond the TE and should not be longer than 10% of the total span. We only use one tab on the Canary because we are trimming for left turn. Bend the left wing tab down 1/32" at a time until the model climbs in a left spiral. Increase turns to the maximum (about 800 on this model) and balance the adjustments above to generate a steep climb and a flat glide. The Canary should fly for 30 seconds or more indoors with a 12" loop of 1/8" rubber, and can zoom above the trees for a minute or more outdoors with a 12" loop of 3/16" rubber. Keep checking that nose bearing for wobble as you fly. Repair with a sliver of hard wood and some Cyano. If your Canary won't climb under 50% power even when balanced properly, add another 1/32" incidence strip under the wing LE and re-trim.

At this point, if your Canary is flying well, let's try to reverse the turn just to see what we can learn. Bend the rudder tab to the right, return the wing tab to a zero setting and try glide and low power tests. If Torque still forces the model left when the rudder is at maximum right setting then bend the left wing tab down again. As this increases lift on the left wing it will force a right bank which will cause a right turn. If you have been successful in flying your Canary both right and left you have really graduated to the next level of flight trim. If with all the above your Canary refuses to fly properly, build a new wing and reglue your tail group or build a new Canary because something is twisted or crooked somewhere.

The AMA Racer

The AMA Racer adds tabs on the stab and right wing to our trim features. These provide a great deal more flexibility in flight profile so we can adjust for longer flights without loss of stability.

Balance the model the same way as the Canary. The CG should be 2" from the wing LE, measured in the center. Check side-to-side balance a bit more closely than on the Canary because of the built up wing. When the model is balanced, try your first glide tests. Don't move the wing more than 1/4" in either direction once the model is balanced. Achieve your glide by bending the stabilizer tabs. If the model dives with the wing as far forward as you can put it, and the CG is in the correct spot, bend the stab tabs up 1/32" at a time. Bend them together or the model will roll to the side. A slight left rudder turn should start you in a spiral climb as you add turns 50 at a time. Just as with the Canary, if the model banks too sharply left, add a bit of down aileron tab on the left wing. If the bank is still too sharp, now try a bit of up aileron tab on the right wing. This acts to reduce lift on that wing and counteract the left bank. Just as on the Canary, you can add 1/32" shim under the front of the wing if the climb is sluggish. Do not add more than 1/16" total. Use stab tabs for the rest.

Again, once you get a good climbing left spiral and a nice, flat left glide, try to reverse the power turn by bending in right rudder and adjusting your aileron tabs for a right bank, ie., down left and up right aileron.

Make notes of the different flight profiles you can get this way. Record all the adjustments and the duration. This is the way to build models that will always perform consistently and will sometimes win contests. Knowing how each adjustment affects the flight profile will also keep your models from flying off the field when the wind changes or you move into a new field with a different shape. Many a model has been lost because it was trimmed for right climb and left glide and the field was too narrow to accept such a wide pattern.

The Courier

The Courier has the same basic trim features as the Racer with the addition of the removable landing gear. This can be removed entirely for best performance or used as a movable nose weight for fine trim. On windy days it is often better to trim your model a bit nose heavy to help in wind penetration, and moving the L.G. 1/4" forward will do this.

The Courier can be flown with either 1/8" or 3/16" rubber. Indoors 1/8" is safer and more gentle, but outdoors the 3/16" will give you a skyrocket climb to over treetop height. Here we must start to exercise some care to avoid a Torque spiral to the left. Add winds slowly and watch that left wing. Also, the chapter on nose blocks and props shows some simple prop hangers that can be used on stick models instead of the molded plastic one. These offer the added feature of adjustable thrust so the Courier can be made to fly in right circles by tilting the nose to the right. This will eliminate the Torque spiral and add an interesting feature to the flight profile. By forcing the model to fly to the right (against the torque) we do not eliminate torque, we simply overpower it by adding a thrust force to the right.

Remember that the torque force is trying to turn our model left by "twisting" it into a left bank. The right thrust we are adding now is simply trying to pull the nose around to the right. Usually 3 degrees or less of right thrust, helped along by right rudder trim, will do the job. In order to maintain a fairly flat circle, however, you may have to start bending your aileron tabs as required. The interesting thing about right power turns in rubber models is that as the motor unwinds torque dies off and reduces left turn pressure thus allowing the model to turn in a tighter right circle. This is what makes for long flights on the field and helps find thermals in the glide. Just a reminder that you bend *DOWN* the aileron on the *DOWN* wing to add lift to that wing and raise it in a turn.

You can also add shims under the front of the Courier wing by slipping them between the 1/8" square pylon retainer and the top of the motor stick. Do not add more than 3/32" of shims.

By trimming these three models for good flight profiles you should have learned a lot about what various trim adjustments will do. The real judge of final trim is the stop watch. Once you have achieved a stable flight profile, time your flights with various small adjustments and the same number of winds. There is some combination of winds and adjustments that will get your model the highest and fly it the longest. While observing these final trimming flights, take a leaf from the basic real aircraft pilot's book. Every airplane has what is called a "Best Angle" and a "Best Rate" climb. The best rate climb will get you the highest in the shortest amount of time.

Since motor run is about the same on all flights you want this best rate, rather than the best angle which is used by pilots only to clear obstacles on takeoff. In other words, just because your model appears to be climbing at a steep angle, it may not be getting as high as it would with a shallower angle but a higher speed. When your model climbs at a very steep angle, it is forced to fly much slower. This optimum speed and best rate climb is unique to each design and may even vary substantially between models of the same design with different weights, trim and surface finish. The stop watch on a calm evening without thermals will be your best judge and after a while you will begin to see when your model is flying too fast or slow.

Later in this chapter we will discuss changing the speed and angle of climb of your model by altering prop diameter, pitch, blade area or rubber motor size. For our basic three models those options are too complex and would defeat our purpose of getting into the air as early as possible with a stable model. After you have had some experience with trimming your three models, try some new trade-offs. If your model seems to be nosing up too close to a stall, trade sideways for up by tightening your climb turn with rudder, ailerons or thrust. This will have the effect of lowering the nose and adding speed. You can also try the reverse by opening up a tight turn.

The effect of adding incidence shims under the front of the wing is to increase the angle between the chord of the wing and a reference horizontal line through the center of the fuselage. Increasing the incidence angle of the wing will add both lift and drag and, will make your model fly closer to the angle at which it will stall. Again you have a trade-off. The highest climb will be attained at some angle close to the stall so we add positive incidence to the wing to make the model approach that angle.

When you have exhausted trim possibilities or wrecked your Courier beyond repair, you are ready to examine the trim techniques for the Condor and other advanced models.

At this point I must mention a problem that besets even the most experienced builder. You are supposed to make only one adjustment at a time. This seems to be like trying to eat only one peanut. Everybody wants to add a little nose weight and just a twitch to the rudder. Unfortunately, as I said before, almost all adjustments are interactive and interdependent so, making more than one at a time can cancel or even reverse the trim you are aiming for. Since everybody is weak in this area, let's just do our best to make one adjustment at a time and to keep notes of what we have done so we can chart the trimming progess and see if we aren't speeding down a blind alley.

Before your first glide test of a more complex model, double check *all* your alignments and check to make sure all your keys, dowels and stops are firm and are where they should be. I've seen even the best competitors lose a model because the D.T. came loose in the climb.

Also make sure your rubber motor is wound tight enough so it won't slop around in the fuselage, and that there are no big knots front or rear. A folding prop with tensioner will hold the motor partially wound or a pin in the back of the nose block holding the prop hook will do the same on a free wheeler. This is a really important step so don' t skip it. We have already discussed how wrong balance can destroy a good flight. Imagine how a shifting balance caused by loose rubber can drive you crazy trying to figure out what went wrong.

Decalage

The last step before your first glide test is to check a factor called "Decalage." This is the angular difference between the wing and the stabilizer. In other words, assuming that a wing chord parallel to the thrust line would be called a "Zero Angle of Incidence," any angle where the front (LE) is up towards the nose would be called "Positive" and where the TE is up towards the rear would be called "Negative." Also, note that Fig. 11-2 shows another angle called the "Angle of Climb." We are going to trade off between these angles to get the best flight. The Angle of Incidence can be controlled with small shims under the stab and wing. These and power adjustments will help control the Angle of Climb. Controlling the Angle of Climb is important because the best Climb Angle for each power setting will give us the highest climb, and the best Angle of Climb in glide will us the most endurance.

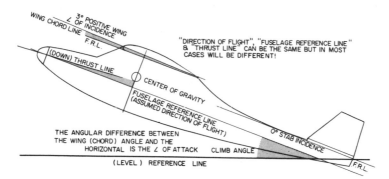

Fig. 11-2. Decalage and angle of incidence.

As your model begins to climb faster, the wing generates more lift and tries for a steeper angle of climb. If that angle gets too steep, the wing will stall and cease to fly. Then your model will simply fall out of the air until it reaches an angle and speed at which it again can fly. This will lose you lots of height and can result in a series of "U"-shaped maneuvers that may end in a crash.

In order to understand the purpose of Decalage a little better, let's assume that both the stab and the wing are able to supply lift. Let's further assume that both will stall (fall out of the air-lose lift) as soon as they reach a certain angle and that angle is the same for both. This stall angle will be reached when the model climbs at a certain angle (Climb Angle) at a certain speed. If we have added some positive incidence to the wing, it will be at a higher angle than the fuselage reference line in Fig. 11-2 and, therefore, will stall even before the fuselage reaches the stall angle. *BUT WE CAN HELP OURSELVES.* All we need to do is put the stab at a *SMALLER* angle than the wing!! As a matter of fact, we can put the stab at a negative angle compared with the fuselage reference line.

Now look at Fig. 11-3. The lift of the wing can be considered to pass through a single point called the "Center of Lift." Since this is in front of the CG, any lift generated tends to rotate our model's nose up because it is pushing up on a lever equal to the distance from the Center of Lift to the CG. The stab is also generating lift but it's Center of Lift is *behind* the CG so it tends to rotate the model nose down. If the wing begins to stall and

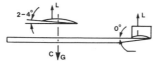

Fig. 11-3. Decalage force diagram.

the stab continues to lift (because we set the stab at a lower angle of incidence than the wing), the model will begin to rotate nose down and will recover from the stall before it falls out of the air. This difference in angular setting between the wing and the stab is called "DECALAGE."

As the model points nose down and picks up speed, the wing again begins to generate lift and rotates the model about the CG to a level attitude. I guess that's why that thing on the rear is called the stabilizer.

The above explanation has been considerably simplified and is not technically correct but it will do as a working hypothesis to allow us to trim a model. Thrust and turn will also affect Angle of Climb and will be covered a bit later in this chapter. In most texts you will probably find references to the "Angle of Attack" instead of the Angle of Climb as above. The Angle of Attack is the angle the wing makes with the relative wind (a horizontal line for our purposes) which from the above would be the Angle of Climb (the angle of the fuselage reference line with the horizon) added to the Angle of Incidence of the wing.

For stable flight the Decalage should be somewhere between 2 and 4 degrees. For those who may have some trouble translating degrees into actual measurements, for every inch of chord, a degree amounts to 1/64" of tilt. For instance, for a 3" chord (on wing *or* stab) a 2 degree angle would require: $3 \times 2 \times 1/64" = 6/64" = 3/32"$. Thus a 3/32" shim placed at the LE of a wing with a 3" chord would give you a 2 degree Angle of Incidence. Most duration models have the wing set at some small positive angle (around 2 degrees) and the stab set at a negative angle (around 1-2 degrees). These angles are later adjusted in small increments to control climb, transition and glide.

Your shims to control Incidence should be large enough to sit solidly on the wing or stab platform and not cause any rocking. For test shims I often use masking tape. I know each layer measures .005" thick and, therefore can control the exact thickness of each shim. The tape is cut in pieces about 1/2" x 1" and layered on each area as required. This is not good as a permanent shim but is fast and easy to use in the field. Plywood is available in 1/64" thick sheets and is a very good permanent shim because it doesn't get crushed over a period of time. For reference, 3 x .005" = 1/64".

Remember, now, your wing should *never* be at a negative Angle of Incidence. If you somehow get there through a series of adjustments, go back and start again.

Trimming The Condor

Insert your motor and put in just enough turns to keep it from sagging. Then balance the model about 1/3 back from the leading edge of the wing. My Condor required a bit of nose weight. You should not require tail weight to balance. Some positive incidence is already built into the wing mounting rails so your are starting with decalage.

Pin the prop hook to keep the motor wound but allow the prop to freewheel. Glide test as described before. Since the wing on the Condor is not movable front and rear, work on the wing and stab incidence to create a smooth glide. The optimum glide path is a sort of "sliding down a hill" descent for a few feet then the model flattens out and "reaches" for the fence in a fast, level attitude.

Assuming your CG is in the right range, if your model is diving, start to add some negative incidence to the stab. Here's another trade-off. You can add negative to the stab or positive to the wing for the same effect in glide tests. However, too much positive in the wing will result in less endurance later on. Try to keep the wing incidence to 3 degrees or less.

Add shims of only 1/64" at a time until you begin to get a fairly flat glide. I generally don't base a lot of my trim adjustments on these first hand glide tests. It's hard to see what is happening in the few seconds of glide, so I just shoot for enough stability to get on to minimum power tests without wrecking the model.

Minimum power is just enough to support the model in level flight for a half or 3/4 circle about 30-40 feet in diameter. This will begin to tell you a lot about your model. Minimum power is about 20% of full turns as shown by your chart. Wind as described and holding the model level, or a bit nose down, allow it to fly from your hand with only the gentle wrist release. Now you can begin to tweak the stab and wing incidence to get a nice, flat circle.

Outdoor high wing tractor models should circle to the right under power. This counteracts the "Torque" force (as mentioned before) exerted by the spinning prop. Torque is a reaction force. In other words it is a force caused by an opposite action. Other forces on the model, ie. lift, drag, thrust, and weight are direct forces. I mention this because the builder must remember that Torque acts to turn the model in the *opposite* direction from the prop rotation. Right hand props on tractor models turn clockwise as seen by the pilot. Therefore, the Torque force wants to turn the wings counter-clockwise or cause a left bank and turn as seen by the pilot.

Since Torque is highest in the first few seconds of flight, when the rubber power is highest and the model is nearest the ground, this is the most dangerous time to have a tight turn.

We also want our model to turn in the glide so it will stay on the field and will turn into a thermal updraft for long duration. These early turn adjustments should be made under minimum power rather than in a hand glide. Before describing the methods for creating a turn, however, let's discuss how we can create direct forces to accomplish these adjustments.

We have already discussed the sled analogy with the Canary and others. This is what I would call a "drag" adjustment because it creates its adjusting force by adding drag to some area which causes the model to want to rotate around its CG. Another type of adjustment is a "weight" adjustment. We have seen this in moving the CG back and forth by adding or subtracting weight. This not only causes the model to rotate, it changes the Angle of Attack thus changing the flight profile. Another weight adjustment might be to add weight to one wing or the other to help the model turn. Added weight on one wing will cause the model to bank to that side, causing a turn.

As you can see, there are a lot of ways to combine all these types of adjustments. The best we can do in this book is to learn what each does, a bit about how they interact and then practice with various models and our trusty stopwatch. With at least six different ways to create a turn we might seem to have a lot to learn but each system has a logical basis so we can work our way through step by step.

Turns

Before starting on turns, note that all the discussion above about right turns refers to models whose wings are at or above the thrustline. Low wing models, like WWII scale, are trimmed to climb left and will be covered later.

Let's start with turns caused by rudder trim. These are the closest to the sled analogy. As we bend the rear of the rudder to the right, the model will start to turn right. Rudder tabs should be placed on top of the rudder so the model will tend to roll the wings flat rather than banking during turns. If your model is stubborn and won't turn right under minimum power even with 1/3 of the rudder turned 1/4" right then we must examine the next factor, "Thrust."

Models with built-up fuselages rather than motor sticks should be checked to align the prop so it operates exactly perpendicular to the thrustline. If you didn't do this and the prop is incorrectly aligned, it will begin to show up now. Therefore, recheck your prop to make sure your thrust is being delivered perfectly straight. Measure on each side from the tip of the prop to the tip of the tail. These dimensions should be equal (Fig. 11-4).

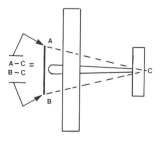

Fig. 11-4. Prop alignment check.

Turns can also be accomplished by causing the model to bank in flight. The model will turn towards the side of the bank. In other words, if the right wing is down, the model will turn right. Banks are caused by reducing the lift on one wing or increasing the lift on that wing. Bending the tab up will decrease the lift. Full sized planes bank by deflecting one aileron down and the other up. I like to increase the lift on the down wing but some stubborn or warped models require both ailerons to be bent in order to get a good turn. Thus, rudder, thrust, wing tip weight, and ailerons can cause turns. Although I don't have real figures, my impression after 35 years of modeling is that stubborn models brought to an expert at the field by a beginner almost always turn out to be either mis-aligned or out of balance, or the platforms and keys are missing. The expert makes a quick check of these factors, corrects what he can, cancels any adjustments put in by the beginner and starts all over again. The moral being that most kits and plan models will fly fairly well with minimum adjustment *if they are constructed warp free and in balance.*

If your model now turns right under minimum power and with some rudder tilt, we can add more power. If it flies straight or still turns left, we start adding thrust adjustments. These are made by tilting the nose block in its nest. In the chapter on props I mentioned that the nose block must be a good, snug fit in the nose and that the nose should be planked and armored with Tyvec or silk. This, of course, would help in reducing crash damage but, even more important, it will help you retain your thrust adjustments throughout the flight. I can't emphasize enough for the beginner how important these platforms, keys and armored areas are. You may have spent weeks on carefully building a model including lovingly finished colored trim, and lose it all because of a wobbly stab, wing or nose block. Unfortunately, many kits, particularly the scale ones, don't show or even mention these most important features. Note that our first, simplest model, the Canarsie Canary, had a bit of extra fuselage wood under the wing to provide a wider, more stable platform.

Also, in the prop chapter, I described a method of attaching small nylon screws to the nose of the model so they could be used to shim out the nose block. This is very effective on larger models (30" and up) and adds insignificant weight. For smaller models, shims are best and I recommend thin plywood (available in 1/64") because it does not crush. You can easily apply double sided tape to a sheet or strip of 1/64" ply and cut it with a scissors right at the field for all kinds of shims.

Thrust

To add right turn to a model, we put shims on the left side of the nose as seen by the pilot. All locations on the model are as seen from the pilot's seat. I have found that almost all the models I have ever built for outdoor FF have required right and *down* thrust. I assume this is due to Torque acting to turn the model left and the very high thrust available at the beginning of the motor run under high winds. For this reason, I usually place my right turn shim at the upper left corner of the nose to add a bit of down along with the right. Here I go making two adjustments at a time after I warned the reader about that. Well, in this case, it usually works out OK, but you can go with a small amount of right thrust and add the down later.

Add right thrust (1/64″ at a time) and right rudder (1/32″ bend at a time) until you get a right turn about 30 feet in diameter under minimum power. If you can't get a turn with 5 degrees right thrust and 30 degrees rudder, you have some warps or imbalance. Start your adjustment checks all over, particularly the perpendicularity of the prop to the fuselage center line. If the model glides right under rudder turn then you probably have a thrust problem in the nose block or the nose of the model. If the model still glides left, check side to side balance and wing and stab warps. If the rear of the stab is twisted so one side is up and the other down, the model will roll towards the high side.

A further check would be to center all controls, glide the model and see which way it banks. If it banks left (left wing down) then it will start to turn left and you have one wing heavier or a warped wing. Certainly you can overcome some warps by forcing adjustments to compensate. I have seen models that fly in a constant left bank with a right turn. You now know enough about adjustments to accomplish this but I hope you also have learned enough not to bother.

Try to remove any warps you find by steaming them out. There is no decent way to remove serious warps at the field. I have seen some modelers rub Cyano glue into a wing TE or LE and hold the wing flat until the glue hardens. This is a "Crap Shoot" kind of fix and should be left to experts or gamblers. If the warps are really bad, take the model home and try another day.

With minor wing warps you can try to compensate by adding aileron tabs. Thin plastic is good or you can apply double stick tape to ordinary kitchen aluminum foil, fold it over and attach to the TE 80-90% of the span from the center. Aileron tab areas should not exceed 2% of the wing area. For instance, on the Condor (12″ x 3½″ = 42 sq. in. area per wing) each aileron tab should be about ½″ x 1½″ (.75 sq. in. or 1.8%).

Do not bend aileron tabs up or down more than 30 degrees. If this doesn't get you the turn you want, then try other adjustments.

As you add power (10% at a time) you will begin to work with the trade-offs I mentioned before. Added power will mean added torque which is still trying to force a left turn. Also, added power means more speed, more lift and more force on the rudder but now the nose is heading up thus changing the Angle of Attack. Don't despair. If we add power slowly and the wind is calm we can spot these small adjustments and make them as we go along.

Power Stall

At about 30-40% power the nose will probably tilt up too high and the model will appear to hang on the prop for a moment, then slide backwards and fall off to one side or nose down and swoop lower until it recovers. This is a power stall and is caused by excessive lift due to speed. This lift tilts the nose skyward and may be the beginning of the dreaded "Phugoid Phollie" so well described by Leon Bennett in many articles. Basically, your wing is generating a lot of lift due to the added thrust and is trying to rotate around its center of lift into a sort of loop. As it noses more and more skyward, it finally reaches a point where the wing can't sustain lift any more (stall country) and it falls. Unfortunately, this happens at the beginning of the flight quite close to the ground because this is where the rubber motor delivers maximum power. As the rubber unwinds, the power lessens and the stall is less likely. In trimming, however, we are starting with very low power so we can adjust for basic stability and we can run into this stall suddenly as we add power.

Almost all beginners with Delta Darts or other simple models wind full right away, get a zoom, maybe a loop and a nose up stall before a swoop to the ground.

Now you can see why I often break my own rule and add down and right thrust together. You can always take away some down thrust if you still have a model.

Washout

Before starting on the next trade-off, let's go back to the chapter on wing construction. There I described a factor called "Wash-out" which consisted of building a very slight twist into the wing tip at the trailing edge so the TE was higher than the LE. This would give the tip a *lower* angle of incidence than the rest of the wing.

With wash-out, as the model approaches a stall, the wing tips will have a slightly lower angle of attack than the rest of the wing so they will tend to stall later than the center of the wing. This means that even in a stall, the model will tend to center itself and not fall off on one tip but will nose down straight thus preventing a spiral or spin. So far, by adding power slowly, we are trying to get a gentle turn to the right. Before we get over 50% power, let's check the flight profile. We should now have enough height to begin to observe the rest of the pattern. Note that there is now a definite difference between the first power burst and the next few seconds of power. As the rubber unwinds, watch the transition from cruise to glide. Rubber power is superior to gas power here because instead of "leaning out" and speeding up as gas engines do just before they run dry, rubber gently dies off allowing the model to level out and smoothly seek a good glide attitude.

Reverse Turn

There is a large body of FF modelers who feel that right climb, *LEFT*

GLIDE is the best adjustment for thermal performance. This causes the model to transition in a sort of "S"-turn that loses almost no height as the rubber unwinds. My Champion Upshot is trimmed this way and is a fine flyer. One drawback of this trim method is the small fields we have in the East. A right-right model will drift with the breeze as it circles and will stay on a narrow field. A right-left model, if the transition turn comes out at the wrong place on the field, will turn towards the tallest tree at the edge every darned time. I mentioned the right-left trim idea at this point because the next adjustment may be useful to those who want to try a reverse turn.

Stabilizer Tilt

Let's discuss an adjustment peculiar to FF models and one of the few that is almost free of trade-off penalties. You may find that your thrust adjustment creates just the turn you would like in the climb but that your glide circle is too wide once the rubber unwinds and the right turning force due to thrust decreases. A whole new way for you to cause a turn is to tilt the stabilizer so one side is higher than the other. This adjustment affects turn *in the glide only*. It's as if nature invented a force just to help out the Free Flighter.

If the stab is tilted so the right side is higher (as seen by the pilot), some of the lift generated by the stab acts perpendicular to the plane of the stab thus pulling it around to the left and turning the model to the right. This force takes over as the rubber unwinds and can help you maintain a tight glide circle without more rudder or aileron deflection. A maximum of 1/32" tilt for every inch of stab span will usually do the job. An easy way to remember which way to tilt the stab is that you want this adjustment to take effect when the model is *high* in the glide and that the model will turn towards the *high* side of the stab tilt (Fig. 11-5).

I think a short review is in order at this point. Table 11-2 shows all the trim factors we have discussed so far, the forces they generate and their effect on flight profile. Obviously, the "Trade-off" column could be

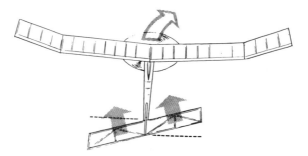

Fig. 11-5. Stab tilt for turn.

Table 11-2. Before Any Trim Flights, Check For: Warps, Wmg, Prop And Stabilizer Alignment.

Problem	Cause	Solution
Dive	CG Location	Reduce nose or add tail weight. Do not move CG more than 1/16 inch at a time and no more than 10% chord total.
Dive	No enough Incidence	Add 1/64 at a time under wing L.E. to max of 4 deg. OR 1/64 at a time under stab TE NEVER SET WING AT NEGATIVE INCIDENCE
Stall	—	Reverse above or add turn
Down Spiral	Side-to-side Unbalance	Check balance and add *small* weight to outside wing if required.
"	Wing Warp	Remove warp or twist wingtip or bend tab down on inside of turn and/or up on outside.
"	—	Add small tab to TOP of rudder and bend to outside of turn.
"	—	Tilt stab or bend elevator tab up on inside of turn.
Too Sensitive	CG Wrong	Move CG Forward
	Trim Factors Under Power	
Stall	Excess Thrust	Add down thrust, Move CG forward 1/32, Add turn, Add side thrust for turn, Higher pitch to reduce speed, larger prop, Less rubber, Longer rubber
Left Spin		Add right thrust, Add right rudder turn
No Climb		Add rubber, Smaller prop, Lower pitch, Add 1/64 inch pos. wing incidence
	Power And Glide Turns Should Be Approximately 30-50 x Span	

infinite in length but, as shown, it will serve as a guide to help you decide on your trim pattern for each model. I can only emphasize again that your model should be as warp free as you can make it and all parts should fit snugly and firmly so adjustments will hold from flight to flight.

Flight Records

Keeping a good record of trimming procedures is as important as building a warp free wing. Without a record you will not be able to follow logically from one adjustment to the next and you won't be able to figure out why some strange things happen when you trade-off one force for another. Also, with a good record you can anticipate problems on future, similar models you might build. I usually set up each new model on a 3" x 5" card, entering source of kit or plan, dates of start and completion, special wood selection notes, weights, number of dope coats and any other pertinent building data. Then I take the card to the field and scribble trim notes and flight profiles each time I fly. By checking this history I can usually predict how to adjust for any field or special condition. Notes on rubber size, turns and prop data are especially useful in fine tuning a model for best performance.

Changing The Power Train

This brings me to a most important part of this chapter and one that requires a bit more study. Early in the chapter when I discussed the three basic models I noted that thrust adjustments were not possible due to the nature of the nose bearing. But couldn't we change the thrust just by changing the size of the rubber motor or the plastic prop? Certainly we could. By working with the power train we can start a whole new series of interactive adjustments that can radically change our lift profile. These were not discussed before because they would have confused the beginner and only slowed his progess into the air.

Modify The Canary

Let's try a simple experiment. Take the Canary or the Racer and remove the 5½" or 6" prop and replace it with the 7" prop from the Courier. You can do this either by rebending or making a new prop hook or replacing the whole hanger and shimming out the nose to hold it. Now, rebalance to accommodate the extra weight and, using the same rubber, return and see what kind of a flight profile you get. It's entirely possible that you may get improved flight times with the larger prop. These first two models were not designed for a larger prop because that would have

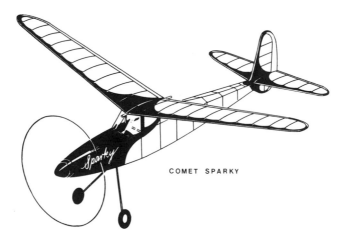

COMET SPARKY

Fig. 11-6. Comet "SPARKY" advanced 32" span model.

114

made them less stable and harder to trim. The smaller prop was able to turn faster which held these two models closer to their optimum speed (remember the arrow?) and therefore made them more stable.

Now you can have some fun by changing the rubber size as well as the prop. Your choices are only 1/8" or 3/16" at this time but you can *lengthen* the rubber motor to see if a longer run will get you a longer flight. Again, the stopwatch will be the judge.

My guess is that the 5½" prop with 1/8" rubber in a length about 1-1/3 to 1-1/2 times the hook-to-hook distance will show the best endurance. In models with stick fuselages and long rubber motors that sag, some designs call for a wire loop called a "can" to hold the motor against the stick. After a few experiments like the above, move to the Condor and start again.

Modify The Condor

First lengthen the 4 strands of 1/8" rubber to about 24". Braid and wind and record the flight pattern which should increase significantly. You had better light the DT fuse during these tests. A great many models are lost when the test of a new adjustments works too well.

The Condor was designed for a standrad 8" plastic prop which has a pitch of about 8". I believe that endurance on this model will decrease if a 9½" plastic prop is used. The larger prop will take more rubber to drive it and, although it will turn slower, the climb will not be as high. *However,* this may not be true for all Condor models. Try the larger prop on yours. Then cut 1/4" off each tip with a scissors and try again. This will probably destroy the balance of the prop but it will do for a test. Add or subtract rubber length until you are getting the best *consistent* flight time according to your history card.

Still using the Condor as your test bed, build a prop using the plastic 1 liter bottle method with a dowel and tubing hub and a free wheeling latch. Design for a 9" diameter with a 12" pitch and a blade 1" wide. Set the 45 degree angle at 2" from the hub center on your pitch gage to get the proper pitch. Try this with a 4 strand, 1/8" rubber motor at 1½ times the hook to rear post length. Braid, wind, retrim and I think you will see your first contest-like performance.

Of course, each of these prop changes will affect balance and thrust adjustments but, if you go slowly, these adjustments will be small and will show up in the first couple of test glides and low power flights. Certainly, changing the prop or the rubber will require changes in the thrust adjustment. A shim change as small as 1/64" behind the nose block can make the difference between a skyrocket spiral climb and a mushy stall.

By first trimming for stability, recognizing the trade-offs involved, then trimming for endurance you will achieve maximum performance and enjoyment.

Differential Stabilizer

The trim adjustments discussed so far should cover almost all beginner type models and, in most of them, will produce stable flight leading to maximum performance. There are a few additional "Fine Tuning" adjustments that may add those important few seconds to endurance. For instance, a very small weight added to a wingtip may increase or decrease a bank just enough to make turns smoother and help glide transition. Also, some modelers will split the stabilizer tabs into two separate elevators so they can be bent individually to different angles. This is called "Differential Stab" and can help you roll your model into a turn. Bending the left side of the stab or the left elevator up will roll the model to the left. Bending right elevator down will add to the left roll tendency. Bending right elevator up and left down will roll the model right.

The AMA Racer is a good model on which to try differential stab. Bend the right stab tab down and the left one up and observe the tight left turn you get. This adjustment should be made in extremely small increments and very slowly, since the rolling motion at high speed can be dangerous.

Low Wing Trim

Although there are few low wing sport models and even fewer low wing contest models, it's important to note for the many WWII and racer scale models that low wing trim is usually *LEFT* climb and right glide. Since you are turning with the torque, extreme care is necessary in gradually working up to maximum power to avoid a left spin. Wingtip wash-out is even more important here and will not usually cost scale points.

There are adjustments unique to scale models because you can't readily change wing or stab angles, and the areas and locations of tail groups on some scale models simply aren't right for free flight. These will be discussed in the scale chapter. Also, when designing your own model or modifying a plan, some other factors come into play. You might have to add area to rudder or make a wing pylon lower or add area to the bottom of a fuselage. These are all factors that help change the aerodynamic characteristics of your model. This chapter covered the trim of models already designed and flight tested.

12

Scale Models

Unfortunately most beginners want to build a scale airplane as their first model. Possibly this is because very few non-scale kits are available in stores and most young modelers prefer the scale appearance. The problem here is that scale models are much harder to build and even more difficult to trim. The airplane is one of the very few technical products that is in general use yet each is designed for a narrow purpose. Today's combat aircraft are each designed for a unique use. These craft are designed to use immense power in a flight envelope of violent maneuvers. Even WWI and WWII pursuit planes were designed to fly on the edge of instability so they would be sensitive to sudden control changes. Except for lightplanes, ultralights, and a few trainers, most modern airplanes if scaled exactly would be almost impossible to trim for flight without a pilot radio control.

We do have scale models supplied by most of the major kit producers and a constantly growing group of cottage industries. The scale model is attractive, lots of fun to decorate with all kinds of details, from Spandau machine guns on a WWI Albatros to a 2″ high pilot busily pedaling a Gossamer Condor.

Some of the kit manufacturers have tried to ease the burden by designing kits that vary a small bit from exact scale proportions and add a bit of dihedral or increase the stab size. Some of these small variations are very important and, although they may cost a few points in a scale contest, they are essential for the beginner.

Don'ts
Let's start with some don'ts before we get into building our first scale

model. Don't start with a Peanut scale model. Because of their small wing area peanuts are difficult to bring in with low enough wing loading for good flight. Almost anyone will have trouble building a model under 10 grams and a beginner may find this impossible. The very small wood sizes required (e.g., 1/20" and 1/32" ribs), and the small areas available for gluing, make Peanut construction tough and tricky. Unfortunately, Peanut kits abound in hobby shops and they are priced to sell as gifts. Put yours on the shelf to save for a later effort.

Don't try a WWI or WWII combat airplane as a first effort either. Since these craft were designed to fly fast, the model's optimum speed is fast enough to make trim difficult.

Do's

Your first scale model should be a high winged monoplane. There are hundreds of designs dating from the 1920's right up to the present that offer all kinds of interesting scale details and attractive lines.

Scale models require construction techniques a bit different from those used for sport or contest models. In this chapter we will treat kit and plan construction separately. Certainly some of the same techniques are used in both, but kits are usually designed for the general public and, therefore, should be modified before and during construction.

Kit Construction Hints

First, choose a scale kit with a wingspan between 18" and 28". This is a good range because you can use some decent sized wood (1/16" and 3/32") and still come up with a flyable wing loading. Once you have opened the kit, checked for all the parts and read the plans carefully, check the general design parameters against some of the factors we know. If a finished weight is given, see if it compares well with our 0.5 gms./sq. in. rule. Check the prop size and rubber against the chart. Refer to the chart for proportions in the design chapter and see how close your kit comes to the ideal. If any of the above is more than 25% above or below good design criteria, consider what you can do to change them.

You can't readily change proportions or dimensions all over the model. You may be able to add a bit of dihedral but that's all. You can certainly change a prop size or save some weight though so let's start with the weight factor.

Most kits have lots of parts printed on sheets of balsa. First, check this printwood for grain and weight. For small scale models the printwood density should not exceed 7 lb./cu.ft. If your printwood is too hard photocopy it, use rubber cement to apply the copy to a new sheet of wood of the proper density and hardness. This can be the most important weight saving in the entire model and can make the difference between good flight and no flight at all. Remember, you will be spending a lot more time building this scale model than most sport models so try to do everything you can to make sure it will fly. I always copy all printwood in case I need a replacement. Of course, after cutting out the parts, remove the paper and rub off the cement.

Also, consider going down a trifle in wood thickness. Sometimes for economy, a manufacturer will print all the wood on the same thickness sheet. You can change to a 1/32" or 1/20" sheet for fuselage formers and, certainly for tail group parts. Next, sand the back of your wood with 250 grit paper to remove fuzz and thin it even further. If the kit was furnished with diecut parts (and few are these days), then sand the back of the sheet with 120 grit paper to make the parts pop out easier. If the diecut sheet is too heavy or hard, pop out the parts, photocopy the scrap sheet and make a new sheet from the copy.

After you have cut or removed the printwood parts, study them for ways you can remove more material. Wing, stab and rudder tips are often much wider than necessary. After all, if the LE is only 3/32" wide you don't need much more for the tips. Remember, the manufacturer is designing his product for the general public and he must work with the maximum strength and ease of cutting so his kits can be built by beginners. To do this he sacrifices a lot of weight and flying ability. At our level we should be ready to change a kit product wherever needed to improve our model. See Fig. 12-1 for hints.

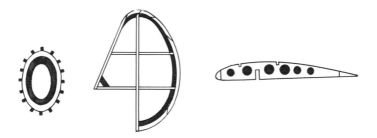

Fig. 12-1. Lighten kit printwood by removing excess.

The sketches show several ways to reduce weight of printwood parts. Note that material should be cut away in curves to eliminate square corners where cracks lurk. Another point to make about printwood is that many kits show curved parts, like wingtips, as one piece. This is poor design since the part may easily crack along the grain when stressed or impacted. Re-make these parts with several pieces as shown so the grain parallels the curve.

Laminated Sections

I believe all tips and other curved or shaped sections should be made by the lamination process as described in the construction chapter. For

119

small models from Peanut up to 24" span, this is mandatory in order to save enough weight to be competitive.

For the larger models, the tremendous increase in strength that the laminated tips offer is equally important. I mold whole tail group shapes, all wingtips and many fuselage areas from thin bass with Cyano glue and balsa with white glue. I find the bass parts much stronger than the balsa and very close to the same weight since the bass in usually 1/3 the thickness of the balsa. Try both methods and use the one with which you are most comfortable.

Wings

Wing ribs should be sliced or cracked rather than solid. You can go from 1/32" solid ribs to 1/16" sliced ribs and still save weight. Also, sliced ribs are really useful in making tapered wings as described in Chapter 6 and shown in Fig. 6-16.

Tail Groups

When building tail groups for scale models another factor comes into play. Our other models all had movable tail parts so we could correct stab incidence or rudder trim for stability. Scale models do now allow us this latitude so we must consider movable control surfaces. Some scale plans suggest leaving a slot higher than the thickness of the stab and tack gluing it until we find the right angle of incidence. This is practical only on some models and may lose scale points if large angles are involved. I find the best solution to this problem is to create a movable elevator and rudder the same as on the original airplane.

The first step in making a movable control surface is to add a strut or stick at the hinge line to give you a closed outline for both parts of the structure (Fig. 12-2). This is where the molded outline really helps because it reduces chances of twist and warp.

Thin copper wire stripped from ordinary lamp cord is perfectly suitable for the hinge. The individual strands of this type of wire work quite well. They run about .005" thick and can be pushed right through most wood down to 1/16" if care is exercised. Where the wood is too thin, just glue the wire right on top of the wood and cover it with tissue. For the purist who

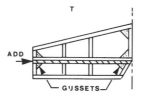

Fig. 12-2. Add a strut to stab to support wire hinge.

wants a less visible hinge and can't bury the wire, a few turns of colored thread (same color as tissue) around the hinge just tight enough to hold an adjustment will do the trick. Take care not to glue the two halves together during finishing or covering.

Note that the same method can be used to create movable ailerons on the wings. Clear plastic tabs for fine trim will be discussed later in this chapter.

Removable Wings

Most scale models are not designed for removable wings. This is OK on Peanuts and other small sizes but as we approach 24" or so we start to get problems of storage, transportation and crash damage. The small models are light enough so the wings won't tear off on a crash but as we start to get to a couple of ounces that monster IMPACT wakes up and roars. Impact is mass times velocity and since we already know that heavier models fly faster, trouble starts at just over 1 ounce.

The solution is called a "Knock Off Wing" and can be built several ways depending on how close to scale you want to be. For many high winged cabin monoplanes, we simply build a one piece wing and hold it with rubber bands hidden in the fuselage. Even tail groups can be attached this way. Sometimes we can use this technique on a low winger. The streamlining can be attached to the wing but it's often really hard to create an invisible joint this way (Fig. 12-3).

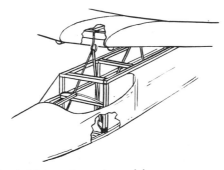

Fig. 12-3. Hidden wing hold down for scale model.

The most used method is to decide on a separation point and build a hook and tube or tongue and slot joint (Figs. 12-4,5). This separation point need not be right at the fuselage side. It's sometimes better to separate the wing one or two bays out so the root fairings flow nicely.

Since the dihedral break will probably occur at the same place, extreme care must be exercised in constructing your "break-away" joint. You must have two solid ribs at the joint and they should be titled so both the

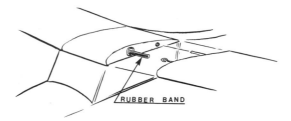

Fig. 12-4. Wire & Tube knock off wing assembly.

Fig. 12-5. Tongue & plug knock off wing assembly.

wing rib and its mating fuselage rib fit flush against each other when the dihedral angle is correct.

To build your "break-away" joint, start with the pin and tube or tongue and box. Build these outside the model just making sure you have enough room to insert them in the wing and fuselage. If required, the dihedral angle is built in now by bending the wire or gluing the plywood tongue as shown. While the wire is in the tube or the tongue in the box, assemble them to the model as the wings and fuselage are jigged in position. At this point in your studies you should be ready to construct assembly fixtures out of scrap balsa and pins to align the various parts of your model. These fixtures are essential if you want scale models that will fly, and are not at all beyond your abilities with a little concentration and care.

When you assemble the wire and so forth, you will also have to construct some packing of balsa sheet and added rib structure and gussets to make sure that all this is solidly mounted against vibration and flight impact. All this should be a good slide fit so the wing will pop off on impact. Now all you need are a couple of .025″ -.032″ wire hooks sticking out of the wing through the fuselage.

A rubber band between the hooks completes the package. Actually, this is another one of those jobs that takes longer to describe than to do.

Removable Landing Gear

Another "removable" feature you might consider is the landing gear. On many WWII models these were designed to retract into the wing. Therefore, using what we just learned, we can build a short piece of tubing into the wing with suitable bracing and bend our wire landing gear to "plug-in." A slight "kink" in the wire or a spring action between two wires will usually work. If the LG is a single strut then flatten the tubing inside the wing to a slight oval to prevent rotation of the strut (Fig. 12-6).

Fig. 12-6. Removable landing gear.

At this point the reader must be asking, "Why buy a kit if I am making all these changes?" Certainly, this point of view has merit. Even if you change a lot of the wood and modify some of the construction though, a kit has already solved many of the engineering problems you will encounter. A kit is also likely to have some lovely decals and vacuum molded parts like canopies, wheel and pilots. I think the scale beginner should try a few kits made by different manufacturers to get a good view of the field. The list of people who sell scale plans is enormous so almost any taste can be satisfied. In general, these plans have been built and test flown so you can be pretty sure that your model will fly.

Let's now go on to fuselage construction where we can save even more weight and learn some new building techniques.

Fuselage Construction

So far we have built fuselages that progressed from plain stick through profile stick then sheet wood and, finally a built up box for the One Night 28, Prairie Bird or Sig Tiger. A very good way for the intermediate builder to start is with a built up box, then add formers and stringers to create the streamlined shape. Most kits use this method although, Guillows and a few others use a keel type technique that will be described in detail later on. So far, we have already covered how to cut away unwanted fat from formers. I don't notch them for the stringers, but simply cut the formers undersized by the thickness of the stringers and lay them right on top as in Fig. 12-1. Most kit former notches are very hard to line up and this method allows your stringers to flow nicely.

Materials

I think a quick review of materials will help here. For fuselage longerons I use the hardest, springiest wood I can find. For everything from 28″ up I use bass. If the plans call for 1/8″ balsa, substitute 3/32″ bass. Fuselage cross pieces are medium balsa. Formers are soft and I often make them from two thicknesses of 1/32″ glued cross grained. This way I can use very light balsa and come up with a very strong part. As long as I am going to discard most of the kit printwood, I may as well make up my new printwood parts as a cross grain laminate. Wing ribs are medium sliced balsa. Wing spars are hard, springy balsa; tips and tail section outlines are laminates of .015″ or .020″ (1/64″ or slightly more) basswood, and fuselage stringers are thin, "C" grain stringy balsa of the type you can't use anywhere else. For planking around nose and wing mounting areas I use very soft (4-6 lb.) balsa and add Tyvec and 1/64″ plywood at the nose, LG mounts and rear rubber peg.

The box fuselage method provides a "skeleton" on which a shape can be formed. Most modern plans call for methods that eliminate the skeleton to save weight and seem to build the fuselage "in the air" out of just the formers. Actually, there are several simple methods for doing this trick and still maintaining a square, straight body.

The Skewer System

This system is deceptively simple. Formers are cut in one solid piece and a square or round hole is drilled or cut exactly in the center. Then the formers are tack glued in position on a dowel or "Skewer." All stringers are added, then most of the formers are cut away allowing the skewer to be removed. The problem here is that the center hole must be exactly placed or else the formers will produce a banana shape. Tony Peters uses this method very succssfully on his fine models. He cuts the formers from thick foam and uses white glue (Fig. 12-7).

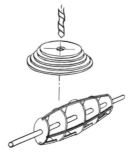

Fig. 12-7. Skewer method.

By the way, when gluing stringers, always alternate. First the top center, then bottom center, then left, then right, etc. Never glue two right next to each other in sequence. This helps avoid warps.

The Keel Method

The more popular "Keel" method is actually simpler and surer. Keels are cut from stiff sheet for the top and bottom then the side outlines. Top and bottom keels are pinned to the board and half formers are glued in place. Then a side keel is glued in and stringers are added. After one side is complete, it is removed from the board, the other half formers are added then the other side keel and the stringers. With some reasonable care, this is one of the best ways to get a light, strong fuselage (Fig. 12-8).

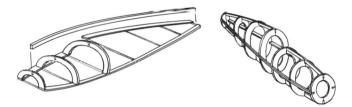

Fig. 12-8. Keel method.

A very fine improvement on the keel method was outlined by Fernando Ramos in his column in *Model Builder* magazine. Fernando credits Al Griffin, a reader, with the idea and proceeds to improve further on it. Basically, you mount a copy of the side view on a sheet of 1/8" balsa or ply and cut slots at each former station. Tack glue the top keel in place on the side view then slide FULL formers in place and glue to the top keel (Fig. 12-9).

A very important caution here is to be sure you cut the notches in the formers *exactly* as required. The notches control the location of the

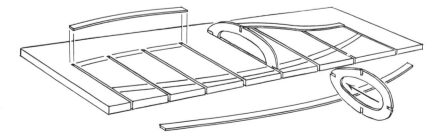

Fig. 12-9. Fernando Ramos' modified keel method.

formers and, therefore, the alignment of the whole fuselage. Here is where the side keels help a lot. Just keep checking that the side keel fits nicely and that the formers match the side view when installed. Keels can be laminated from either balsa or bass as described earlier. This adds strength with very little weight penalty. Also, this method allows for alternating the stringer assembly for better warp control. Keels should be designed so they extend beyond the formers the same amount as the stringers. For instance, 1/16" square stringers would call for keels 1/16" x 1/8" with 1/16" notches, in the formers only, at the keel points.

If your fuselage has been built with notched formers for all stringers, you should scallop the formers between stringers so the tissue flows nicely along the length of the fuselage. This can easily be done using 240 grit sandpaper on a dowel.

So far, we have only covered the basic construction methods needed to make decent flying scale models. The really careful work and planning comes in during the assembly and the added touches like windshield, windows, landing gear mountings, canopies, scale engines, etc. An entire book this length would hardly be enough to describe all the things that can be done to enhance the appearance of a scale model. Fernando Ramos and others, in many articles over the years, have described hundreds of these techniques. I will cover some of the basic ones here but the best reference for the serious builder are library magazine files.

COVERING

Before covering your model you should begin to consider exactly what extra scale features you want to include. The beginner should keep it simple. Thin tape or ink lines to indicate control surfaces and canopy frames, a photocopy of an instrument panel glued to the proper former and folded paper, tubing or dried grass to cover the LG wires will do it. Later on, the beginner can indulge in rigging wires, complete cockpits, wire wheels and more. However, even the simplest scale features will require some planning. Let's start right at the front end.

A tilted nose block is really unsightly on a scale model. Use the movable sheet metal rear bearing to adjust thrust (Fig. 12-10). The thrust

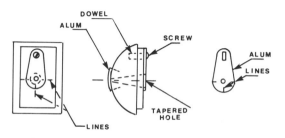

Fig. 12-10. Thrust adjustment method for scale models.

bearing hole is drilled in the nose block then tapered towards the rear with a rat tailed file. A dowel is pressed into the nose block and a small sheet metal screw is inserted in the dowel. The sheet aluminum or steel bearing plate is slotted for the screw and drilled for the wire hook. It should also be carefully marked for dead center location as a reference. Now you can adjust thrust by loosening the screw and sliding the bearing plate up or down or rotating it sideways. The tapered hole allows the rubber hook to tilt thereby changing the thrust line.

Another neat idea from Fernando Ramos by way of Louis Garami is the rear driven free wheel prop shown in Fig. 12-11. The wire wrapped

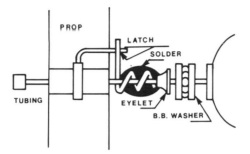

Fig. 12-11. Rear drive free wheeler allows prop replacement.

around the shaft and soldered to it and the eyelet drives the latch from the rear thus allowing the prop to be slipped off by just removing the piece of tubing in front. Don't worry, the friction against the latch keeps the prop from flying off.

Props are not counted in scale point judging so you can use whatever flies best. Mark Fineman's index card props are perfect for scale. They can be painted to resemble the original and will take a lot of abuse. Carve your nose block to resemble the original but make sure you have a good fit in the nose of the fuselage. A tiny piece of screening glued to an appropriate hole in the nose block nicely simulates an air intake or coarse gauze doped gray will stiffen up to do this. If the scale engine has protruding cylinders, drill holes for these before completely forming the nose block. Techniques for simulating cylinders will be covered later.

I use a lot of bond paper and card stock on scale models. Areas around engine cowlings and cockpit coamings need some stiffening under the tissue. A piece of bond paper glued right over the stringers does a fine job. Card stock is also very useful for wing fairings and landing gear covers.

The last step before covering should be a careful check of all parts to be sure you have built in ample support for all scale details and movable or removable parts. Test the glue joints of all gussets and planked areas.

Now examine your model and imagine the covering being applied strip by strip. See if there are any areas where the covering has no support at the end of a strip. For instance, when fuselage stringers reach the rear you may need a piece of scrap between them to support the tissue. Perhaps you have used sliced ribs and not put a bottom support or whole rib at the root where the knock off wing ends. Fill all these spots with the softest balsa, sand and dope, then begin covering.

Covering

Covering is the same as described earlier. Most scale models have streamlined sections that have to be covered in strips. Dry tissue will not curve in two directions (like the surface of an egg) without wrinkling. For example, areas where the fuselage tapers towards the rear and also has a rounded cross section or where the wing thickness tapers towards the tip and still has an airfoil shape a bit more care is required.

For fuselage strips, lay the tissue on an area between two stringers and, with a soft pencil, mark the line of the top stringer in the section. Using a new blade or a piece from a double edged razor, cut the tissue just under the pencil mark. The tissue grain should be along the fuselage from front to rear. Now place the tissue strip carefully on the top stringer so it doesn't overhang at all, stick it to that and the next stringer using thinner. Work along from front to rear in short steps smoothing, stretching and aligning as you go (Fig. 12-12).

If the stringers are very close together you may be able to cover three with one strip. However, any space larger than 3/4" or so may create wrinkles if covered by a single strip. It is almost impossible to get this type of wrinkle out by water or alcohol shrinking because the tissue is folded in both directions and it doesn't shrink as much across the grain. If your model is large enough to cover with silkspan (36" or more) then you can cover wet and use much wider strips. After your strip is glued down, trim the overlap from the bottom or next stringer as close to the stringer as you can. Keep this up all around the fuselage.

Try to plan the operation so the last strip ends on some open area so the trimming will be easier. If you have to trim the last strip where it meets another, work very slowly with a very sharp blade and in good light so you don't cut the tissue right next to the stringer. On some strips you may have to add some dope to the upper stringer that has tissue on it. Use a small brush and thinned dope.

When planning the fuselage covering you may want to add a thin, narrow (1/32" sheet) panel along the top or bottom where your last strip meets the first one. This will simplify the trimming operation.

This method will give you a smooth covering but will show a double thickness of tissue on most stringers. This is not too unsightly and can be covered up later when you apply colored dope. Most contest scale models are color doped to hide the structure and to look more like the original

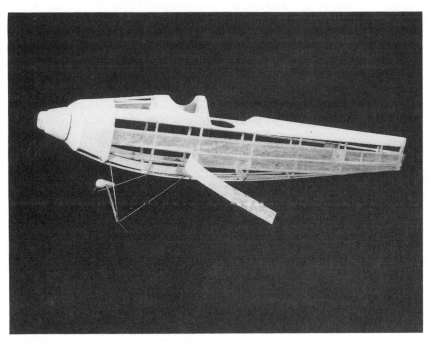

Fig. 12-12. Covering a fuselage in strips.

which may have been a metal or plywood skin. If you have a fuselage with a lot of curves, consider covering it with wet #00 silkspan. Even if it is smaller than 36″, I used this on several models in the 22-30″ range with very little weight penalty and a savings of lots of time.

Air Brushing

Once your scale model has been covered and the tissue shrunk, we get into a whole new area of modeling skill. If you are really serious about scale appearance and want to compete you will have to learn something about air brush spraying. There is equiment available at low cost (around $25.00) that will include a simple Badger Airbrush system that is powered by a can of propellant. This is probably the only reasonable way to start.

The next grade up will be a small compressor system that will run around $100, but you may find that the propellant can system has a lot of other disadvantages. Small pattern, irregular pressure and inadequate pattern control all contribute to make the job harder. Perhaps you can pick up a good spray system at a garage sale or, maybe come up with some household uses to justify it. Any way you do it, a good air spray system with a decent capacity gun will immediately increase your modeling pleasure while enormously enhancing the quality of your work.

Once you start spraying and get some experience in handling the gun, you will replace a lot of brush work on all types of models.

The above doesn't mean that you can't color dope scale models with a brush. But even with the most careful brush doping you will pay a severe weight penalty and have a very difficult time getting a smooth, even finish. For colors, the system used in model railroads has all the shade variations you will ever need. These paints are called Floquil colors and can be bought in a powder that mixes well with nitrate dope. Beware, Floquil colors do not mix with Butyrate dope.

At this point you should begin to do some chemical testing. There are Magic Marker type pens that come in a huge variety of colors and are also compatible with dope. Some can be painted right on top of a doped area and others can go on bare wood or tissue and can be doped over. For instance, India inks can be applied over dope and in most cases will not run. "Marks-A-Lot" is one type of alcohol soluble markers that can be used under dope. Sometimes the dope has to be applied in an almost dry coat (this is where spraying is important) to keep the marker ink from running.

I mention the above because color trim is a good way to add appearance points to your model, and the ability to paint on stripes or lines without spraying more dope is important. The new generation of ruling pens allows even a novice to draw fine lines without blots. If you find the right marker you can use it directly or pull out the flat wick, soak it in alchohol for 12 hours, squeeze it out with a pliers and use the result with brush or spray. A few hours of experiments with different, inexpensive and easily available markers will repay itself many times over by adding a whole new dimension to your modeling fun. It will also build confidence in your own skills and may result in some altogether new methods that no one else has tried.

A visit to a large art supply store is a must for the serious scale builder. There are tapes made by "Chartpak" that come in widths down to 1/64" and a variety of colors. There are acetate or rub-on shapes, arrows, circles, etc. that can be applied to simulate panel lines, controls, exhaust stacks and others. Every time I go to one of these places I discover another clever item that can be used in scale work.

Here I *must* emphasize the proper technique for any handling of chemicals.

ALWAYS READ THE LABELS FIRST AND OBSERVE ANY RECOMMENDED SAFETY MEASURES

ALWAYS OPERATE IN A WELL VENTILATED ROOM AND WEAR THE APPROPRIATE FILTER MASK

AT THE FIRST SIGN OF ANY DISCOMFORT LEAVE THE AREA — SEEK FRESH AIR AND/OR CONSULT A DOCTOR

Harry Higley's book, "There Are No Secrets," is about the best for any beginner. You will be surprised at how easy it is to become a passable spray painter and you will have added a new skill to your repertoire.

Before starting on scale features, a few words about where to find them. The source list shows several places to find scale documentation. These suppliers can furnish photos and even dimensioned drawings of many features of your model. These documents are very important in winning scale points so, before actually building your scale engine, refer to some source for the appearance and size of the original. Some scale buffs visit airports and antique fly-ins to photograph scale subjects.

Also a word about scale itself. You may find the phrase 1/12 scale or 1/24 scale in a book or plan. This simply means that the model is 1/12 or 1/24 the size of the original. This is important in choosing the size of your features. Too often some builder puts what works out to be an eight foot high pilot in the seat of his otherwise perfect P-40. If your model is 1/12 scale then 1" on the model equals 12" or 1 foot on the original. Thus a six foot pilot would be 6" high.

Of course a lot of this scale documentation is needed before you start assembly, but most kits and plans the beginner would build have this work already done. The scale features, though are worth a little extra trouble.

13

Scale Details

I have devoted a separate section to scale features because for some modelers, these provide the most building enjoyment and satisfaction. Certainly good scale features can earn you points in a contest and they are really fun to show whenever the gang gets together for some "Hangar Flying." I remember spending quite a bit of time working out a way to get a swivelable, shock absorbing tail wheel into my RN Fleet Biplane. When I finally worked it out (Fig. 13-1), I couldn't wait to show it off to the other fliers. I mounted the wire strut in a short tube then glued a piece of sponge rubber to the former to allow the strut to bounce and swivel.

A good builder may spend as much time on scale details as all the rest of the construction, but the trick is to make these details as realistic as possible without adding significant weight to the model. We'll cover some techniques that will help but the most important of these methods requires the builder to learn a whole new process called "Vacuum Molding."

Fig. 13-1. Swivel & bounce tail wheel.

Vacuum Molding

As I have said before, don't be scared off by something that seems technical or difficult or requires a new piece of equipment. If you intend to follow this hobby for a while, then learning new techniques should become part of the fun. Vacuum molding is about as hard to learn as prop forming and not as hard as wet covering, both of which you have done already.

Basically, there are thin plastic sheets sold which can be softened when heated. Sig sells Butyrate sheets in various thicknesses and Acetate is available from many plastic suppliers. Perhaps you can check your local phone book under "Packaging" for people who do "Blister Packaging." They will probably be willing to give you all the scrap you need and my guess is they will be glad to give you lots of technical help. Just bring along a model.

Fig. 13-2 describes a simple vacuum molding setup you can build. Ron

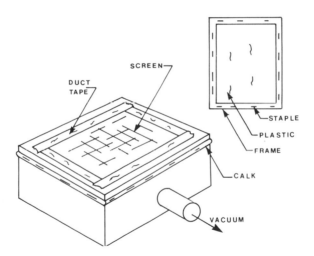

Fig. 13-2. Simple vacuum molding box.

Williams, in the April 1976 issue of *Model Builder,* shows a complete plan for a unit that can be built in a couple of hours and will last for years.

For those unfamiliar with the process, it is based on the ability of some plastic sheet materials to flow when properly heated and to assume the form they are stretched over. First, carve a wood form for whatever you want to mold. Note that the plastic can't be removed from the form if it has any undercuts. These are areas where the part is narrower on the bottom than on top. You will have to figure out how to split your master form so there are no undercuts. (Remember, I *told* you this was a problem

133

solving hobby.) Sometimes as with a pilot, you may be able to carve a full pilot, split it, insert a 1/4" thick spacer to allow the material to flow over the full shape then insert the pilot in your base as shown, so only half projects for each molding cycle.

The plastic sheet is then stapled to a forming sheet that has been provided with an opening just slightly larger than the mold. Heat the assembly to about boiling temperature and watch to see when the plastic sags. At this point, press the assembly over the mold while the vacuum continues pulling. This process takes a bit of practice but the device and the technique are your's from then on.

Some simple parts (e.g., canopies and wheels) can be molded without vacuum. Cut your forming sheet from 1/8" ply to be just 1/4" larger around than your mold. Heat the plastic and force it over the mold without a vacuum. While this is certainly feasible, I think that as long as you are going to the trouble of carving molds, then the added accuracy of the vacuum molded part is certainly worth the small additional effort. Unfortunately, a vacuum molding toy once made by Mattel is no longer available. I have been haunting garage sales for years looking for one.

Molds can be used over and over, so pilots, guns, wheels, engines, canopies, seats and whatever else you can imagine will become part of your library of molds to use on scale projects. I guess each builder will have to decide how far he or she wants to go in adding scale details to a model. A quick visit to a local airport will give you a dozen new ideas. Remember though, weight is still our enemy so keep track of the weight additions as you get more and more realistic. Tony Peters keeps a big junk box of all kinds of little plastic and metal pieces that can be cut up and used as parts of scale details. He recently found a hair bow that was made of a material that is absolutely perfect for a WWI radiator front.

Cyano Molding

Jim Kaman, who illustrated most of this book, uses a unique Cyano

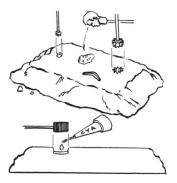

Fig. 13-3. Jim Kaman's Cyano molding process.

glue method to make small molded parts. As shown in Fig. 13-3, Jim carves a pilot or buys a small doll and simply presses it into a glob of clay. He then drips Cyano glue into the female impression until he has a nice, even coat all over the inside. After the glue dries hard (don't use accelerator), he peels out a perfect replica in thin, transparent, paintable, strong Cyano.

These parts can then be treated the same as half shapes furnished in kits, or vacuum molded by you. With care you can reuse the clay mold, or destroy it, clean off the clay with lighter fluid and make another when needed. Another interesting feature of this process is the ability to make a part thicker in cross section than the original. Just push the master deeper into the clay and fill the depression with Cyano. I've tried small gears and wheels and I'm sure this would work very well for cowl bumps, exhaust stacks, machine guns and other parts too tiny for vacuum molding. Screws of the proper sizes are perfect engine cylinder masters.

Paper Mache

Some of you may remember the above from Kindergarten. Here's where you finally get to use it for something practical. Jim Kaman again deserves credit for the idea. Buy a doll, save from a kit or scrounge up a concave shape of your pilot or whatever. Spray the inside with Silicon release then push in one layer of paper towel (the kind with the bumpy surface). Work some 50-50 Elmer's glue into the paper with the bristles of a hard brush. Push in another layer, work in some more glue and allow to dry. Paint and decorate to order.

Carved Foam Parts

Another Tony Peters' gem is his method for carving super light parts from foam and making them dope proof. Tony covers the parts with tissue adhered with 50-50 white glue and water. If the parts are curved (as on wheel pants) he slits the tissue around the curve, the same way as in Fig. 7-6 for wingtips. Tony then folds the tissue around the curve and covers the overlaps with white glue. Add a coat of white glue overall and you have a hard, shiny, dope proof surface.

Grass As A Scale Detail

Here's another good idea. My English friend, Jeff Anderson goes out each summer and collects a big box of different sized grass stems. He looks for the types that are hollow, mostly weeds and puts them aside to dry.

After a few weeks he has a large collection of pieces of fairly stiff tubing in an almost infinite variety of diameters. The stuff can be doped in color, strengthened with Cyano, cut, glued and bent. It can be used for landing gear fairings, cockpit coamings, gun barrels, antenna masts, control horns, turnbuckle covers for rigging and, even tires. Just soak the green stem in hot water, bend it around a disk, allow to dry and paint black.

The uses for grass stems are as broad as your imagination. I suggest them because only a little effort will provide some very light components.

Engine Cylinders

Engine cylinders are another area where you can try a lot of ideas. Williams Brothers makes a fine series of cylinders for any sizes of models. These are molded in plastic and are quite light. Grass stems again "crop" up as another alternative. Take a long stem of the proper diameter and wind two strands of heavy carpet thread in a tight, shallow, spiral along the outside surface. Wipe a thin layer of glue over this and when tacky remove one strand of thread. This will leave you with a nicely finned cylinder that can be cut off to length. With some care you can make a whole engine from one stem in one operation (Fig. 13-4).

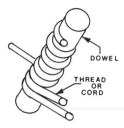

Fig. 13-4. Scale cylinder using dowel, cord and glue.

Exhaust stacks, spark plugs, rocker arms and other engine parts come out of balsa scraps, broom straws and wire. A bit of gray mixed with the black dope gives a nicely weathered appearance. Some builders I know will spend a week on just the engine and the results are usually well worth the effort.

Engine Turned Finish

In the 1920's and 1930's, a few airplanes had aluminum cowlings with a turned or spun finish. The Spirit of St. Louis and the Ryan ST are examples. This can be easily simulated using kitchen foil. Just tape or rubber cement the foil to a sheet of wood, mount a new, round pencil eraser in your drill chuck and press lightly on the foil in a carefully lined up pattern.

Fuselage Markings

Here's another neat trick. With the easy availability of photocopy machines that reduce, you can type some signs like "Pilot Tube" or "Inspection Panel" or even the pilot's name and kill signs on a fighter, reduce them to the appropriate size and copy them right on to tissue by taping the tissue to the photo paper before feeding it in to the machine. Cut out each sign and glue carefully in position with a minimum of dope (the dope will sometimes make the copy run, so be careful).

Canopies And Windows

Canopies and windows are probably the toughest parts to make and a poor job will certainly detract from scale appearance. Good windshields are easy with the following technique. After proving out the exact size with a piece of paper and the "Cut-and-Try" method, wet your paper pattern lightly and lay it on the plastic. It will stay where you put it. Now cut out the pattern and add two or three "Points" (Fig. 13-5). Fit these points into thin razor slits in the balsa or bond paper coaming in front of the cockpit. A drop or two or glue will hold it there. Now choose a piece of string or grass stem of the proper diameter, dope it silver, black or the color of the fuselage and, using vinyl cement (so the dope won't bleed) glue it around the base (Fig. 13-5).

Fig. 13-5. Windshield assembly.

Some windshields have several vertical and horizontal braces as well as a top rim of rubber. For the flat braces, bond paper can be color doped and glued in. A nice touch is to make small pin holes in the paper to simulate rivets.

For front windshields on cabin airplanes try the thin plastic used for sandwich bags. Glue in tightly all around even if the shape is complex. Then heat *carefully* with a hair dryer and it will shrink drum tight.

Canopies on WWII fighters are a problem. Unless you can find a commercial one that can be modified, you will have to mold it. Some builders will buy a kit just for the molded canopies, wheels, and other plastic parts, and will completely rebuild the model while discarding all the wood. Actually canopies are the easiest part to mold. Most have no tricky bends or bumps and can be made in one piece. If your canopy had framework inside, just glue a piece of string or thin wood over the mold to produce a bump, then insert a strip of bond paper doped on both sides into the appropriate place.

Canopy mounting can sometimes be done with points like windshields. If this is not practical, here's another method. Very carefully cut a piece of bond paper that is a tight fit around the outside bottom of the canopy and a good fit on the fuselage between formers or stringers. Glue in the bond paper before covering and carefully cover with tissue trimmed to the same outline. Now your canopy can be nested just inside the bond paper pattern. Try never to use Cyano glue on canopies or windows. The vapor that comes off as the glue dries will fog the clear plastic. Also, regular Acetone model glue is difficult to apply without getting some on the plastic. There are several Vinyl type glues around that are used for furnitues. These dry clear and without stains. Elmer's glue also dries clear and is strong enough for this purpose.

Side windows are another tricky subject. For Peanuts and other light, small models the Saran or sandwich wrap idea is best. Just make sure you heat very lightly.

For larger models, a full window assembly will look really good. First make sure the edges of the window area are covered with tissue or color doped. Then construct a window frame from bond paper. Dope it or cover with tissue on *BOTH* sides. Now add your thin plastic window. Glue in and shrink. If you are building a larger model and want to be even more accurate, mount a sheet of plastic in a frame to stretch it smooth, then sandwich it between two bond paper frames. Glue the window assembly into the model slightly recessed from the side of the fuselage (Fig. 13-6).

Window curtains, magazines (reduced in a photocopy machine), pilot and passengers, seats and headrests are all good ideas but each carries a weight penalty so take care not to exceed our weight guidelines.

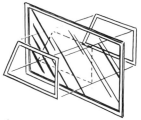

Fig. 13-6. Slide window with frame.

Instrument Panels

Instrument panels are another area where imagination is the key. For Peanuts, a flat photocopy will do. For more detail consider individual instruments drawn with pen (colored as required) and glued to 400 to 600 grit black, wet or dry sandpaper to simulate black crackle finish. Walnut shelf paper may be perfect for a 1930's biplane panel. For the real buff, cut

138

a piece on 1/16" ply the size of the panel and drill holes the size and location of the instruments. Lay a sheet of your vacuum forming plastic on top, heat a round ended piece of metal rod and press it into each drilled hole thus forcing the plastic to bulge up slightly as it would over an instrument. Now draw your instruments on a white sheet. Mount the white sheet under the plastic and glue a sheet of 400 grit black paper with appropriate holes over the top (Fig. 13-7).

Landing Gear

Landing gear is another area for scale detail. Again, grass can be used to simulate oleo struts or fairings. Wheels could be a chapter in

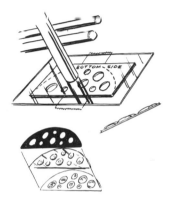

Fig. 13-7. Control panel details.

themselves. Hungerford wire wheels are wonderful but expensive. Williams Brothers makes some nice plastic old timer wheels and, with a few lines or pieces of thread glued to the clear plastic disks, they simulate wire wheels fairly well.

Some builders make their own wire wheels creating a fixture to hold a short tubing hub and another for the balsa rim. Then they wind silk thread between the two for spokes. This is tricky and time consuming but adds a lot to an old time model and, the fixtures are re-usable. A neat way to make a rubber tire for any kind of wheel is to pick a dowel of the proper outside diameter and insert it into the neck of a small balloon. Now roll the balloon back over the dowel (as you would a stocking). When you have the appropriate thickness of tire, put a couple of drops of Cyano on the rubber, slice it off, paint black and you have a lovely scale tire.

Wheel retainers are also simple. Instead of bending the wire up in an unsightly manner, slip a piece of aluminum tubing over the wire and hold it with a bit of Cyano. On larger models, drill a hole crosswise through the aluminum tubing and make a tiny cotter pin from soft wire. For bungee

139

cords on Old Timer models, try the very thin elastic thread available from dress making stores. This can be colored with magic marker.

Tony Peters has a good method of avoiding crushed fuselage members caused by hard crashes, while still allowing the LG to flex in a very realistic manner. He simply attaches the front leg rigidly to the fuselage and allows the rear leg to slip into a small slot in the fuselage. When the gear flexes, the rear leg just slips in a bit deeper.

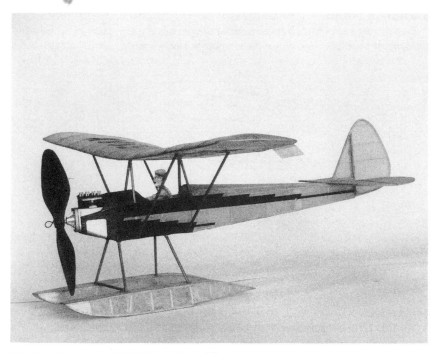

Fig. 13-8. Tony Peters' 20" "Heath Parasol."

Decals

Decals are furnished with almost all scale kits. The trick is to apply the decals with no wrinkling. "Solvaset" and "Micro Sol" are two products sold by railroad model suppliers for this purpose. They break down the surface tension of the water and allow the decal to smoothly follow the contour of the base surface. Spraying Testor's "Dull Coat" on top will almost make the decal disappear into the tissue but before trying these chemicals, test them on your surface both doped and undoped.

Rigging

Oh, the wind in the wires. Those romantic biplanes of WWI dog fighting in the skies over France. I don't think I have ever met a modeler

Fig. 13-9. Bob Bender's Peanut Santos Dumont "14 Bis."

who didn't want to build a Spad, a Nieuport or an SE-5 someday. Probably the idea of all that rigging has frightened off many who wanted to try one. As I mentioned before, you can use very thin elastic thread available in dress making stores or silk thread from the same source. Avoid ordinary household sewing thread because it will sag or shrink with changes in humidity. For small models sew the thread right through the wing panels. For larger ones, glue small "U" shaped wires to the wings and run the rigging through them. Grass turnbuckles are a nice touch too.

Struts

Interplane struts or wing support struts should be removable wherever possible. Make them of light wood or even paper so they will break away in a crash and not puncture the wing. They can easily be plugged into small pieces of tubing glued inside the wing if you prepare the areas before covering. Wherever possible, without adding too much weight, try to have thin balsa or card stock under the tissue where struts rest. If the struts are not plugged in they should be lightly glued with Elmer's (which dries clear) or a drop of rubber cement or a dab from a glue stick. These are not as strong as standard model glues so, like an electric fuse, they will pop loose before damage is done. Since most model wings are self supporting, struts and rigging are only cosmetic and should be as light as practical.

141

Cabanes

A cabane is the structure that supported the wing in some of the old time airplanes. In the actual airplane, the cabane was tubing, wire or hard wood. In your model the cabane should be wire inside a balsa sandwich or wire covered with paper to simulate tubing. All wire cabanes should be built in fixtures to insure that the wing will be straight and square when mounted. The best idea for a parasol model is to build the cabane and wing center section as a unit. Mounting of the cabane to the fuselage and wing center section should be engineered with care before you cover. The struts should be attached directly to a main longeron with epoxy, then braced and gusseted solidly. The same is true at the wing joint. Use gussets or hard balsa strips to join the cabane to the LE and TE.

Since scale models do not usually have movable wings or tail surfaces, we can't use all the techniques discussed in the trim chapter. We can get some help from movable elevators and rudder and can certainly adjust thrust. I would start trim procedures with a forward CG (around 25% of the chord from the LE) and some downthrust. Also, many modelers use clear plastic tabs added to wing TE's near the tips. These can be bent just like the tabs on the Courier or Condor. Propeller and rubber choice is very important on scale models. Build your nose with a slotted block and try several props. The difference in performance between an 8″ diameter x 11″ pitch and, say an 8½″ diameter x 10″ pitch may surprise you.

For the equation minded, here's an interesting scale for scale models. A rough estimate of the duration that can be expected of a particular scale model can be calculated as follows:

$$\text{Duration (sec.)} = 50\text{x [rubber wt. (oz) / total wt. (oz.)] x}$$

$$\text{wing area (sq. in.) / total wt. (oz.)}$$

In conclusion, if you turn into a real scale buff, the number of scale details you can put in your models is almost infinite. The best way for you to get more ideas is to visit an air museum or your local airport and look around, take pictures and make sketches. You will find all pilots interested, informative and eager to "Hangar Fly" with you and discuss lots of planes they have flown. The Appendix lists several sources of scale data which will help further. I think it is the small detail that is fun to make and will get your buddies' attention at the field, as well as getting you contest points. Fire extinguishers, flight bags, luggage, a 45 pistol strapped to the pilot's chest in a Flying Tigers P-40, an observer with binoculars in the right seat of a rescue plane, reduced size sectional charts, the list is endless. But always remember the weight penalty for every detail added.

14

Other Scale Types

I wish space permitted a detailed analysis of the many scale types and events that are available. Perhaps a future volume can cover these in detail.

Peanut Scale

Peanut scale is defined as a scale model with a span 13″ or less or fuselage length 9″ or less. There are no other restrictions. With an average chord of 2″, this 26 sq. in. wing area needs a really light model to get down below our recommended wing loading. You will need all you have learned about construction and covering to get that weight of 8-10 grams.

1/20″ sticks for spars and longerons, 1/32″ sliced ribs and formers or even 1/64″ sheet will be needed. Mount your tissue in a wood frame, shrink and dope it in the frame, then apply. Vacuum or Cyano molded details and ink lines to simulate panels and control surfaces will add great detail appearance with little weight penalty.

Although I prefer scale models 16″ span and up, in order to get a decent wing loading while using reasonable wood sizes, the profusion of Peanut kits and plans available indicates that the rest of the world loves the little beasts. They certainly are fun, easy to pack and can be built in one piece using simple construction techniques. Be sure to keep that weight down and trim in very calm air.

Profile Scale

I think profile scale offers the most fun for the smallest investment of time and effort. With a span of 16″, *single surface* covering and a motor stick with only a one side "ghost" fuselage, these little beauties can

143

Fig. 14-1. Langley Peanut Nowlen Aero kit.

weigh as little as 5 grams and turn in flights of over two minutes. At wing loadings of .15 to .25 gms/sq. in. you are almost into indoor country, yet able to simulate scale appearance and flight.

I form the entire wing, fuselage and tail outlines from 2 layers of .015" x 1/32" bass molded with Cyano. Profile scale models, called "No-Cal Scale" are perfect for trying experimental designs. You can build, trim and fly a pusher, canard or flying wing over a long weekend. The light weight permits lots of no damage crashes and the open fram e and motor stick allow for a large range of adjustments.

FAC Scale

Designed as a fun alternate to AMA Scale, the FAC rules allow for wheels up configuration and hand launches. Bonus points are given for all kinds of model types that are more difficult to build and fly like biplanes, canards, and multi-engine. The FAC "Mass Launch" event is the closest a modeler can come to being in a rodeo. FAC groups compete all over the country and have events for Greve and Bendix racers, WWI and WWII fighters, Golden Age models, No-Cal Scale, Peanut and many others, all run in a friendly, fun-fly atomosphere.

Bostonian

Strictly speaking, Bostonian is not really a scale category. Limited to a 16" x 3" wing, and requiring a fuselage capable of enclosing a block 1½" x 2½" x 3", Bostonians are intended to create a "Fun Scale" event. They are required to look like a scale model and must include LG, windshields and ROG capability but are designed to display some "Charisma" in a whimsical fashion. Flight duration is multiplied by the "Charisma Factor" which is up to the contest director, so the fun begins right there.

Jumbo Scale

Defined as over 36" span for a monoplane and over 30" span for a biplane, Jumbo Scale can really return fun for effort. Able to carry a wing loading up to .8 gm./sq in., you can pile on all the scale details you can imagine, add lots of planking, gusseting and hard wood spars and still have a floater. The flight of a jumbo starts to resemble a real airplane including long rumbling takeoffs.

Fig. 14-2. Don Ross's 16" "Heinkel" profile.

15

Duration Models

Again, space limitations preclude expanded coverage of all the various types of competition models but, I feel the following comments will help the reader in choosing the right type of model and flying it with success and satisfaction.

Embryo
Designed as a beginner's event, the Embryo is a 16" span model with a 6" plastic prop. There are several kits available, they all fly well, and are capable of long glides in thermals. Most Embryos have completely adjustable wings and tails and, with a nose block adjustable for thrust, can be an exciting first contest model. Extra points are given for details like wheel pants and exhaust stacks, so some scale fun is included.

P-30
I think this is the best type of model with which to enter competition. Built to a minimum airframe weight of 40 grams, the P-30 allows for good sized wood (3/32" longerons and spars, 1/16" ribs) and its span of 30" delivers a good wing loading and plenty of thermal opportunity. The 10 grams of rubber allowed provide a 30 second motor run that will really get you up there. The plastic prop won't teach you much but it's very easy to convert a P-30 to a sport model with a 12" folding prop which will turn in 4 minute flights. I have found my various P-30's very forgiving and capable fo demonstrating a wide variety of trim conditions. You will need a good DT system and you can try several flight profiles with the same model.

Coupe d' Hiver

Translated as "Winter Coupe," this event was designed to make a high tech competition model fly off a small field in winter conditions to a 2 minute max. Coupe is probably the best way a beginner can get into a higher level of competition. Rules call for a minimum airframe weight of 70 grams, a fuselage cross section of 3.1 sq. in. and only 10 grams of rubber. This is a very low power to weight ratio (10 gm. rubber to 80 gm. total wt. = 1/8 or 12.5% ratio where most designs call for 25%).

Coupes use large folding props up to 18" diameter and a short, fat motor. Spans run around 36" and with a chord of about 4½", area is 162 sq. in. with a total weight of 80 grams, the wing loading is very close to our magic .5 gms./sq. in.

With Coupes we begin to see some high tech composite construction, complicated front ends that fold the prop based on torque rather than tension (Montreal Stop), Turbulators, Invigorators and Variable Incidence Tails. All the above are important to the serious competitor and help get that precious few seconds of glide that make a string of maxes.

Montreal Stop

Using a basic "Z"-hub, this often complex mechanism is actuated by the torque of the rubber. It provides a much more positive prop stop at a controlled point on the torque curve thus insuring better transition from power to glide. The only commercial Montreal Stop available is from Starline International and is called the Simplex MK-2. Bob Hatschek has designed a much simplified version he calls the Hiborks that can be made with bent wire. Plans may be available from the National Free Flight Society.

Turbulators

Air passing over a wing tends to stick to the surface in a thin layer of air called the "Boundary Layer." Turbulators are thin strips (1/64" -1/32") of balsa or heavy thread placed at the 5% and 15% chord positions to help break loose the boundary layer so the wing develops more lift. Some Wakefield models with solid balsa wings have a sawtooth like pattern cut about 1/32" deep into the LE to do the same job. Although Turbulators are becoming popular they are still somewhat experimental and, like any other major adjustment, require complete re-trimming of the flight profile.

Invigorators

After the boundary layer is broken up it sometimes re-establishes itself too soon. Invigorators are very thin (.005" - .010") strips of tape. Three or 4 are placed at equal intervals between the 40% and 80% chord points (back from the LE), and sometimes at the stab 40% point. I have also seen invigorators used on props where they are said to eliminate "Prop Whistle" which may reduce efficiency.

Variable Attitude Tails

The ability to change the deflection of the rudder or stab in flight can certainly help in competition. Climb almost straight out, then increase stab negative incidence and rudder turn for the slower glide and thermal hunt. Some use the slap of the folding prop against the fuselage to release a trigger. Others use multi-function timers. The latest method is to use the changing torque of the motor as in the Montreal Stop. George Xenakis attaches a wire yoke to the rear motor peg which is allowed to tilt slightly in an elongated hole. The twisting action is then translated into stab or rudder movement.

Mulvihill

Limited only by a 300 sq. in. wing area restriction, Mulvihill models have it all. Spans up to 55", props up to 26" and 1/4 pound or more of rubber make these graceful behemoths the most spectacular and satisfying of all rubber models. With motor runs of 2 minutes and more,

Fig. 15-1. The author's potent P-30 from Pharis kit.

Mulvihills need vast fields and calm air. Most Eastern contests have a 7 AM mass Mulvihill launch and a dozen of these clawing for altitude at the same time is a sight to remember. There are only two kits available but magazines and plans services can furnish lots of modern and old time winners.

Wakefield

This is the most prestigious of all model trophies was created in 1907 by Lord Wakefield and, except for the war years, has been awarded each year in an international competition. Wakefield team members must first win regional then national competitions in their own countries so you can be sure the real cream rises to the top of this group.

Modern rules call for a 190 gram minimum airframe weight plus a maximum of 40 grams of rubber. Total projected area of wings and stab must be between 263.5 and 294.5 sq. in. These specs dictate a very efficient model capable of almost straight up climb and awesome glide. All the above high tech building and controlling techniques appear in Wakefields. I only know of two kits that are available. The Tilka from FAI represents the state of the art configuration while the Wake-up from Champion is a bit more like a classic design. Both are for the advanced builder and are superb kits including the very best wood and fittings. Of course, it takes more than a fine model to win, which brings me to our next subject.

Competition

Winning a model contest takes about the same level of dedication as winning any other tough race or contest. The first requirement is practice. You must be able to fly your model in all kinds of conditions and knowing exactly what the model will do. Some contests are won by the guy who builds the night before and enters after one test flight but not many. Build a completely reliable model that will repeat its pattern every time. Key all surfaces and pre-test rubber. That will get you up to the flight line. The last factor is the ability to pick the proper air.

Lift

Lift or thermal activity is what stretches flight times and, the ability to find thermals is what wins contests. Thermals are gently rotating donut shaped columns of air that rise from the ground right up to the clouds. They can be found over macadam roadways or concrete runways. As thermal rises it pulls in cooler air and therefore, can be detected by a slight temperature drop or, maybe a chill on the cheek. Light Mylar streamers mounted on long poles will suddenly rise indicating a thermal front. Modern competitors use thermisters and recorders to identify thermal patterns. The best advice I can give the beginner is to discuss thermal finding at contests and try to launch right behind the old timers while observing the various conditions.

16

CO2 And Electric

I feel this book would not be complete without some description of the CO_2 and electric motors available for small, rubber power-type models. Great advances have been made in these power sources over the past few years. They are now reliable, safe, silent and powerful enough to fly reasonable sized models.

CO2

The CO_2 motor works much like the old time steam engine. Instead of using the expansion power of hot steam, the CO_2 motor uses expanding carbon dioxide. The energy comes from cartridges that are used to make seltzer and they can be purchased in most hardware stores. The gas is released from the cartridge through a special loading charger into the small tank supplied with the motor. As the prop is flipped to start, the piston rises and pushes open a ball valve that admits gas from the tank. The gas pushes the piston down until it passes an exhaust port which allows the gas to escape.

These tiny motors are easy to install and service and will stand an awful lot of abuse. They can provide enormous pleasure even on a small field. Just carry the charger in your back pocket, fill, launch, fly, then retrieve and charge again with no winder, stooge or rubber lube. While not as powerful as a rubber motor, their speed is infinitely adjustable from barely ticking over for a long run to a quick burst for a high climb.

CO_2 motors are made by Brown Jr. in America and Telco in England. I have had lots of experience with the Brown engines and find them extremely rugged and reliable. The Telco products seem to vary a bit more in quality but both types operate satisfactorily and can be handled by a beginner.

Davis Diesel makes some conversion units that turn a gas engine into a CO_2. These are available for both .020 and .049 engines. But I feel that these and the larger electric motors are substitutes for gas engines on larger models and should not be reviewed in this book.

Electric

Now that batteries for small electric motors have come down in weight and the motors have become more powerful, these units are practical for small models. The HY-70 system made by VL products is a geared motor weighing 1¼ oz. that can fly a model up to 30" span. Delivering only slightly more power than a CO_2, but weighing almost twice as much, the small electric motor is limited in flight capability but not at all in the fun it provides. Clean, quiet, safe and chargeable in a couple of minutes; electric is another treat for the sport or scale flyer.

Both electric and CO_2 power lend themselves well to scale types that don't have long fuselages to house rubber motors. How about some of those WWII types with the short, stubby front ends? The extra weight of an electric motor might be perfect for balance. Twins, pushers and flying wings are good subjects. Two motors can be run off the same tank or battery even though the props rotate in different directions! I'm working on a Seabee flying boat with the motor in the rear and the batteries in the nose.

There are lots of kits that can be easily converted to electric or CO_2. A particularly good one is the Guillow's Arrow. If built lightly it is a fine, stable performer. Carl Steinberg has one that tops one minute consistently and occasionally produces two minutes in still air.

17

Designing Your Own Rubber Model

By now, you have had a chance to practice construction and trimming techniques on at least four models. If you have gone on to build a P-30 or some scale models, then you have experienced success in both building and flying. Perhaps you are ready to design your dream model or just want to modify some existing design to appeal more to your particular taste. This is not as hard as you think and does not require lots of aerodynamic education. If you stay within the general areas shown on the design sketches then you can come up with an infinite series of shapes and arrangements.

Now that you know how to build a tapered wing or stab with sliced ribs, you can design one for your model without having to lay out a lot of different sized ribs. Elliptical tips or specially shaped rudders are a breeze with your laminating techniques, and oval fuselage cross sections are equally easy.

One thing to avoid at first is the "Universal Model" that everyone envisions somewhere along the way. The "Universal Model" is one with lots of interchangeable wings and tail groups and 3 or 4 fuselages that will make up for everything from a floating contest model with a pylon through a 1930's bipe and a zippy low wing racer. It's certainly possible to do this but each will require its own trimming arrangements and, probably, none will fly as well as a simple model designed for one purpose.

Fig. 17-1 shows typical proportions for a high winged rubber model. This can be a cabin or a pylon type. These generally accepted proportions are based on span because the beginning designer usually decides what span he likes, or what span will fit his board or box comfortably, and then

152

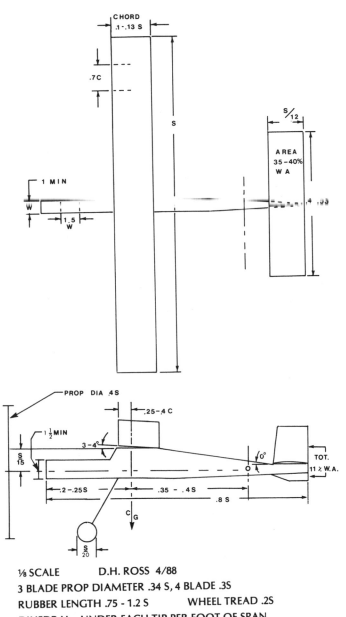

CHORD
.1 -.13 S

.7 C

S

1 MIN

W

1.5
W

S/12

AREA
35 – 40%
W A

.4 .05

PROP DIA .4 S

.25 – .4 C

1½ MIN

3 – 4°

S/15

0°

TOT.
11 % W.A.

.2 – .25 S

.35 – .4 S

.8 S

C G

S/20

⅛ SCALE   D.H. ROSS 4/88
3 BLADE PROP DIAMETER .34 S, 4 BLADE .3S
RUBBER LENGTH .75 - 1.2 S   WHEEL TREAD .2S
DIHEDRAL: UNDER EACH TIP PER FOOT OF SPAN
     HIGH WING 1¼"   MID WING 1½"   LOW WING 1⅝"
     TWIN RUDDERS: EACH 65% SINGLE AREA

Fig. 17-1. Monoplane proportions.

153

proceeds to build a model around that. For sport models, that is as good a way as any to start.

Note that the drawings in this chapter are 1/8 scale to provide a finished span of about 28″. You can use this to measure dimensions not listed. Proportions are given as fractions, decimals or % to give you practice using all three, so be careful to multiply or divide correctly. For instance, 1/20 S means divide span by 20. 20% S or .2 S means multiply span by .2.

A more accurate method for general proportions would be to use wing area since we talked a lot about area and loading in previous chapters, but I feel that might add confusion at a stage where the beginning designer needs all the confidence he can muster. After all, it's difficult to spend hours designing a model then, perhaps weeks building it and worry all the time whether it will fly or crash dismally.

Let's work with span first and assume that we design for an Aspect Ratio between 7 and 9. Aspect Ratio is simply the span divided by the chord so a P-30 has an Aspect Ratio of 30/4 = 7.5. A high Aspect Ratio provides the most lift with the least drag. This will give you long gliding flights with a low sink rate. A low AR gives a swift, high climb but somewhat less of a glide, so as we wrote before, you must pick your own trade-offs.

Propeller diameter is given in the sketch as .4 times span. This may not always agree with the propeller figures shown in the prop chapter and is intended only as rough guide. The prop chapter figures are more accurate.

Average Chord

Up to now, we have made all our wing measurements using the Chord of the wing as the dimensions from the front of the LE to the rear of the TE. This is correct as long as the wing is a rectangle. When we get to tapered, swept or elliptical wings this figure must be modified to accommodate the particular shape. For a tapered wing, the Average Chord is the area (we have previously discussed how to find this) divided by the span.

The Average Chord will be needed when figuring the proportions of the various model types. Many of the basic dimensions start from the CG which is shown as a fraction of the average chord.

The Table accompanying the sketch will help you with other configurations, such as low wing or twin tail. A check of the dimensions of the Condor will show that they are very close to the illustration. If you deviate much more than 10% from most of these proportions, you will probably have to trade-off something else somewhere. For instance, the figure of .30S from the CG to the nose is based on the fact that the rubber motor is a substantial fraction of the weight of the model (25%) and therefore, the CG should be close its center. This gives you a long nose which is not bad to have on a rubber model. Of course you can cut the nose down but you may have to add weight to properly balance the model.

As a general guide, rubber should weigh about 25% of total weight including the rubber. For instance, if your airframe weighs 45 gms. *without rubber* then add 1/3 of that in rubber or 15 grams of your best braided power source to make the total 60 grams so the rubber will be 25% of that. (15/60 = 1/4 = 25%). If we check out P-30 we find that the rubber (10 gms.) is only 20% of the total (40 gm. airframe wt. + 10 gm. rubber = 50 gm. all up, and 10/50 = 1/5 = 20%). Rubber in P-30 has been restricted to make the model a better small field contest item and to run the small plastic prop. A 12" prop on a P-30 (.4 Span according to our chart) would probably require 15 grams of rubber to drive it.

As your design progresses, you will begin to ask yourself questions about the actual "Engineering" of the model: "How far apart should the ribs be? What size should the longerons be? How high the pylon?" These are, of course, impossible to answer in total detail. As a matter of fact, there are no "Best" answers. Just as in flight trimming, there are a lot of trade-offs and many "Right" ways to do things. Table 17-1 will give you some general ideas. Add strength by increasing wood sizes where you think your particular model will need it. Use hardwood (bass or spruce) and ply sparingly but, don't be cheap and try to cut too many corners. Nicely radiused gussets not only look good, they save weight too. The table should be enough of a guide to get you started and, as you progress, meet other fliers, and read the magazines you will pick up most of the tricks and probably invent a few of your own.

A good way to try out new designs is by building an all sheet balsa model. This works well from about 18" to 36" span. We have gone over the various techniques for all balsa construction and these will allow you to play around with prop size and pitch, and rubber size until you prove out your ideas. You can save a lot of time this way and will be able to try out your ideas for unique configurations.

Design Purpose

Before starting any new design, carefully list its REQUIREMENTS and their PRIORITY. For instance, do you want a biplane for appearance and are you willing to give up a bit of glide too? How much strength will you give up to reduce weight? Would you be willing to fly the model ONLY in calm morning air and build it like an indoor job? The trade-offs start right here.

In the next few pages I will cover a series of designs and will list some of their advantages, disadvantages and points of special interest. Some of the basic material was developed originally by Charles H. Grant in his many articles and in his book "Gateway To Aero Science," some by Frank Zaic in his year books, and some by William F. McCombs in

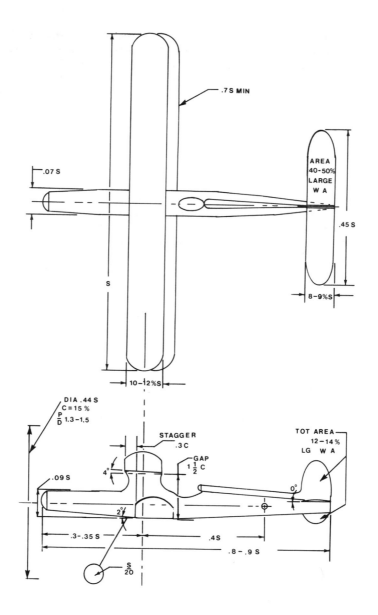

.7 S MIN

.07 S

AREA
40-50%
LARGE
W A

.45 S

8-9%S

S

10-12%S

DIA .44 S
C = 15 %
$\frac{P}{D}$ 1.3-1.5

STAGGER
.3 C

GAP
1 $\frac{1}{2}$ C

TOT AREA
12-14 %
LG W A

.09 S

4°

0°

2°

.3-.35 S

.4S

.8 - .9 S

$\frac{S}{20}$

⅛ SCALE   D.H. ROSS 4/88

Fig. 17-2. Biplane Proportions.

"Flying and Improving Scale Model Airplanes." All these should be in
the library of any serious model designer.

My ideas don't always agree exactly with the above experts but represent a sort of distillation lightly peppered with original thought. Almost all the material in the design sketches has been sort of "Common Knowledge" since William Winter's, "Model Aircraft Handbook" was published in 1943. (Yes, I still have a well worn copy.) and has provided designers and builders with basic starting blocks for decades.

Before rushing to the drafting board, consider some of the other basic design parameters. The size of your building board, the size of your field and the size of the trunk of your car are legitimate concerns and should be factored into design equations before the first line is drawn.

Biplane

Let's go on to Fig. 17-2 to explore a model type that I think everyone has in his "Someday" box. I saved the Beautiful Dess plan from 1963 until 1983 and must have mused over it a hundred times before I got the chance to build it. So far, every flight has paid back my patience with interest. I owe Charlie Wood a great debt of gratitude for all the pleasure his design has given me.

Biplanes were originally conceived to solve a construction rather than an aerodynamic problem. Early airplanes made of wood and fabric were actually a lot weaker in structure inch-for-inch or pound-for-pound than our stick and tissue balsa models. While we have no trouble supporting a wing of even 9:1 aspect ratio, the old timers needed wire rigging and posts to hold their structures together under flight loads. It's easy to see that a box structure, as on a biplane, is more rigid than a single, cantilever wing. Short span for storage and low aspect ratio for maneuverability are also bipe advantages.

Of course, drag is the downfall of the bipe. That extra wing doesn't pay for itself with enough lift to offset its drag. The extra construction and alignment work can't be ignored either but after all of the above, bipes are still romantic and attractive.

For good biplane performance we can't simply stick another wing somewhere above or below the first wing and start trimming. Since most of our design calculations are based on wing area we must remember that in a bipe we have to consider the area of *BOTH* wings.

Also, the relationship between the two wings on a bipe can be critical to stability and performance. The "Gap" is the vertical distance between the wings and should be at least 1.5 times the chord. Biplane wings should also be "Staggered" by placing the lower wing 1/3 of the chord to the rear of the upper wing.

Compare Figs. 17-1 and 17-2 to see where biplane and monoplane factors differ. Note that tail moment and prop areas are larger on bipes, to accommodate the extra wing area.

There are two schools of thought about biplane wing incidence. One described by Charles Hampson Grant is that the upper wing should be at a higher angle of incidence than the lower so that it will stall first. With a positive stagger (upper wing forward of the lower), as the upper wing stalls, the lower whose center of lift is *behind* the CG will induce a moment (turning force) that will tend to level the model. In this case the lower wing is doing a bit of the job of the stab as described in the part of the trim chapter where we covered decalage.

William F. McCombs feels that the lower wing should be at a higher angle because it is operating in the downwash of the upper wing and has less lift.

I tend to agree with Mr. Grant because I design first for stability and then for performance. Also, I think that proper gap and stagger will help eliminate downwash problems. If bipes are your thing then start with the basic parameters and a degree or two of positive decalage. Then, put the stop watch to work while you vary the angles slightly without changing prop, rubber or winds. Fig. 17-3 shows the pitch forces in action at the stall point.

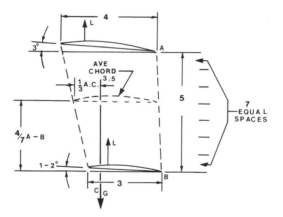

Fig. 17-3. How to find biplane CG. (Note: Average chord for any wing is equal to area divided by span.)

That extra wing on a bipe does complicate the problem of finding the CG but with a little persistence, a sketch and a very little math we can come fairly close before we attempt a flight.

A biplane can have equal wings that are directly in line or equal wings that have either positive or negative stagger. Or, it can have unequal wings in either of the three arrangements above. Wing shape is not a factor because we can now find the average chord of any wing.

With equal wings directly in line the starting CG would be 25% - 33% back from the LE of the average chord.

With unequal wings of either negative or positive staggered, we first find the average chord of the *combined wings* and its location. First

158

make a scale sketch of both wings showing average chord of each, the gap and the stagger. Fig. 17-3 shows a scale drawing of a bipe with upper wing average chord of 4", lower of 3", gap of 5" and stagger of 1". The average chord of the two wings will be located a distance above the bottom wing equal to the proportion between the two average chords. In other words, the proportion is 4 to 3 so the average chord is located 4/7 up from the bottom as shown. The length of the average chord is the distance between the lines drawn from LE top to LE bottom and TE top to TE bottom. Now locate the starting CG at the usual 25-33%. I refer to starting CG because final trim may move this 5% or so in either direction for best flight times. When calculating the wing area on any model, use the whole projected wing including the part that goes through the fuselage. Negative staggor would be worked the same way.

Canards

Canard, meaning duck or lie in French is the generic term for an aircraft whose small wing is in front of the main wing. The origin of the term is lost in antiquity. Some think a canard in flight resembles a duck and others that the French refused to believe that the Wright Brothers had flown and thus labeled their achievement as a "base canard."

I feel the canard is a highly underrated design type that was discarded in the early years for purely mechanical reasons and is only now achieving the popularity it deserves. The Wright biplane and many other early fliers were canards but the heavy engines of WWI made the pusher canard configuration harder to balance. Also, the very stable nature of the canard was considered a disadvantage in combat where violent maneuvers are required.

Today we have many ultralights, attack bombers, executive jets and sport lightplanes designed as canards.

The canard advantage is the very steep climb angle it can attain, its gentle stalling action, ease of turn trim by simply tilting the front wing, and better prop protection as a pusher. I think these are overwhelmingly important for the beginner. Canard models are very forgiving and can operate stably over a wide range of prop/rubber combinations. So far, rubber powered canards have not won many contests but I think they are one of the best sport types around.

Figure 17-4 shows the general proportions for a canard. Rubber and prop parameters are similar to those of a tractor model but trim is a little different. The rudder on a canard is not as effective as the rudder on a tractor model because it is so close to the CG. Turn trim is accomplished by tilting the front wing down on the side you want to turn towards. Since the prop is behind the CG, right and left thrust adjustments are reversed. Tilt the right side of the block *as seen by the pilot* out from the nose to get LEFT turn and reverse for right. UP and down thrust are the same as a tractor model. Note in the sketch that the main wing is set at zero

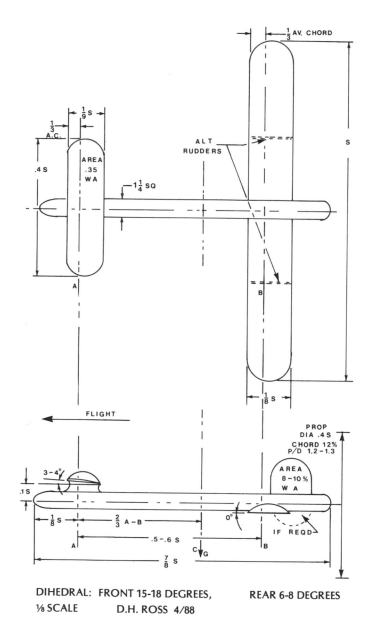

DIHEDRAL: FRONT 15-18 DEGREES, REAR 6-8 DEGREES
⅛ SCALE   D.H. ROSS 4/88

Fig. 17-4. Canard proportions.

incidence and the front wing is at 3-4 degrees. This is proper Decalage for a canard.

Most canards are pushers and should be built with left hand props to make winding easier. A left hand prop rotates counter clockwise as seen from the rear of the model. They can be carved by reversing the diagonal on the tip of the standard prop block or, when formed on a cylinder, tilt the center line 15 degrees to the right instead of the left as on a tractor prop. I have found sketches are no good to describe this. You will have to make your left handed prop while constantly comparing it with a standard prop to be sure both blades come out right.

To find the starting CG on a canard lay out a scale sketch of the side view showing average chord of each wing and their true fore and aft locations. Mark a spot, (A), 1/3 of the AC (Aerodynamic Center) back from the front wing LE. Also mark a spot, (B), 1/3 of the AC back on the rear wing. Your CG is now 2/3 A-B back from point A.

Sometimes a canard will show a disappointing desire to spiral in the glide after the gyroscopic action of the rear prop is gone. The only cure I know is to add a small fin under the tail. Use an area of 5-7% of the wing area, and increase if needed.

My experience with canards has been very good. I have several all sheet models of about 16-18" span that never fail to entertain in small field flying. They perform consistently with almost no damage under all kinds of conditions. My larger canards fly in a stable pattern in both calm and windy conditions and have surprisingly flat glides. The ease of trimming for tight turns helps fly them safely from the smallest fields.

Flying Wings

Of all the possible model types, flying wings best typify the ultimate design challenge. I think everyone wants to try a "wing" someday and I also think everyone is a bit scared of the design and its trim problems. In full sized aircraft, flying wings have not yet fulfilled their potential in either civilian or military capacities.

On first analysis, a wing should be extremely efficient since it can totally eliminate drag from fuselage or tail members. The famous Northrop wing of the 1940's is a fine example of an almost pure wing design. If featured engines and passenger compartment completely enclosed in the wing structure and had no stabilizing tail. Introduced with high hopes, the Northrop wing never fulfilled its original promise. Flight tests showed it was quite sensitive to CG shifts and its load carrying efficiency over long distances was lower than conventional designs.

While wings do eliminate lots of drag, their lack of pitch stability and the need for some arrangement to correct this often more than negates any savings. Most flying wing models employ a considerable amount of sweepback and, also some reflex at the trailing edge to provide pitch stability. With sweepback between 30 and 60 degrees and 10-15 degrees of TE reflex you are giving up a lot of flying area. Sweepback is the angle between the LE of the wing and a line perpendicular to the fuselage.

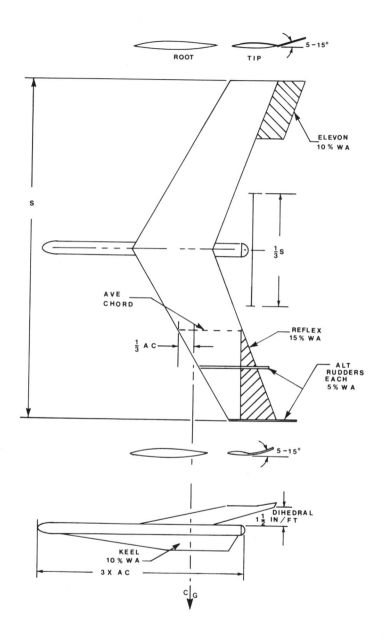

ELEVON OR REFLEX CONFIGURATION
⅛ SCALE   D.H. ROSS 4/88

Fig. 17-5. Flying wing proportions.

Reflex is the angle between the up slanted TE and the chord line. Figure 17-5 shows these factors. Another way to accomplish the same effect as reflex is to add elevons to the TE near the tips. Add elevons with each having 10-15% of the total wing area and tilt them up 6-10 degrees. These are shown dotted in the sketch. I think the most stable airfoil for a flying wing should be a symmetrical one. This is shown as the root airfoil in the sketch.

Another problem for rubber powered flying wings is the need for a long fuselage sticking out from the wing to house an adequate motor length. This often adds to the pitch stability problems. As if the above wasn't enough, wings seem to have very little directional stability. Any gust will cause the model to rotate around its CG.

All the above problems seem to do is cause modelers to work harder to solve them. And solve them they certainly do.

Over the years I have seen scores of successful flying wings and each one has more than repaid the designing and trimming effort.

Figure 17-5 shows the conventional layout for a flying wing. The sweepback and relexed TE handle the pitch stability problems. The bottom keel reduces the directional stability problem and the high dihedral and rear rudders add roll resistance and directional control. Many wings of this type do not employ a bottom keel. I think it can be very helpful in trimming. My young friend David Aronstein flies an indoor wing with a small rudder (6% of the wing area), right up at the nose. This seems to provide very good directional stability.

You should also try a delta wing. These are stable and capable of incredible climbs although, the glide is not so hot. Just draw a triangle with a 60 degree angle at the point and a height 1½ times the width. Add reflex or use the whole rear as an elevon and start trimming.

Table 17-1.

Model Size	Peanut	16-24"	24-36"	Above 36"
Longerons	1/20 - 1/16	1/16 - 1/8	3/32 sq.	1/8 sq.
L.E.	1/16	3/32	3/32	1/8
Spars	1/20	1/16 - 1/8	1/16 - 1/8	3/32
Stringers	1/20	1/16	1/16	1/16 - 1/8
Ribs	1/64 - 1/40	1/32	1/16	1/16
Formers	1/64 - 1/40	1/32	1/16	1/16
Sht. Tip	1/40 - 1/32	1/16	3/32	1/8
T.E.	1/20 x 1/8	3/32 x 1/8	1/8 x 3/8	1/8 x 1/2
Molded Tip	2 Strips	2 Strips	3 Strips	4 Strips
Spruce	1/64 x 1/32	1/64 x 3/32	1/64 x 3/32	.020 x 1/8
Rib Spacing	2/3 Chord			

Fuselage cross pieces and uprights 1/12L or 1½ minimum.

All dimensions in inches.

Fig. 17-6. The author with his Cyrano flying wing.

Figure 17-6 is a picture of me with another type of wing. The Cyrano, designed by Barnaby Wainfan and printed in *Model Aviation,* is designed for the P-30 event. It is a "Plank" or rectangular wing with no sweepback at all. It has lots of dihedral and a reflexed trailing edge on an airfoil designed by Barnaby. This model was so successful it tied for first Place at the NATS in its first year.

It's hard to say which type of model will give the most satisfaction. I've tried some types because they looked good and some others "just to get them out of my system." I think all modelers should try new types. They add to the challenge but they also add to the spice.

Whatever your modeling goals, I hope this book will help you to "slip the surly bonds of Earth," as I have done, and find the special enjoyment of the world of rubber powered model airplane flight.

Appendix

Table A-1. Determining Propeller Tip Angle.

Tip Angle Degrees	P/D	3	4	5	6	7	8	9
18	1.0	6.16	8.21	10.26	12.32	14.37	16.42	18.48
20		6.90	9.20	11.50	13.80	16.10	18.40	20.70
22		7.66	10.21	12.77	15.32	17.87	20.43	22.98
24		8.44	11.26	14.07	16.88	19.70	22.51	25.32
26	1.5	9.25	12.33	15.41	18.50	21.59	24.66	27.75
28		10.08	13.45	16.81	20.17	23.53	26.90	30.25
30		10.95	14.60	18.25	21.90	25.55	29.20	32.85
32	2.0	11.86	15.81	19.76	23.71	27.66	31.61	35.56
33		12.31	16.43	20.54	24.64	28.75	32.86	36.96
34		12.80	17.07	21.33	25.60	29.86	34.13	38.40
36		13.79	18.39	22.98	27.58	32.18	36.77	41.37
38	2.5	14.83	19.78	24.72	29.66	34.61	39.55	44.50
40		15.93	21.24	26.56	31.87	37.18	42.49	47.80
42		17.10	22.80	28.50	34.21	39.91	45.61	51.31
44	3.0	18.35	24.47	30.58	36.70	42.81	48.93	55.05
45		19.00	24.33	31.67	38.01	44.34	50.68	57.01

Follow the top column (prop *radius*) in inches across to your prop size. Then go down the column which shows pitch (distance traveled in one revolution) to the closest number to the desired pitch. Travel across to the left column to get tip angle of prop or forming block. Note that the values for 1.0, 1.5, 2.0, 2.5 and 3.0 P/D ratios have been underlined. 12.31 is a P/D of 2 for a 6 inch diameter prop and 30.58 is nearest to a P/D of 3 for a 10 inch diameter prop. Note that each P/D occurs at the same tip angle for any sized prop.

ORGANIZATIONS

Academy of Model Aeronautics (AMA)
5151 E. Memorial Drive
Muncie, IN 47302
(765) 287-1256
Insurance, Model Aviation
Magazine, Club Listings

Flying Aces Club
3301 Cindy Lane
Erie, PA 16506
Newsletters & Contests

Kits & Plans Antiquitous
Morris Leventhal
1788 Niobe Ave.
Anaheim, CA 92804
Collectors Newsletter

National FF Society
Fred Terzian
4858 Moorpark Ave.
San Jose, CA 95129
Newsletter, Symposiums

Society of Antique Modelers (SAM)
209 Summerside Place
Encinitas, CA 92024
OT Modelers Society

PUBLICATIONS

Aero Index
73 Charlton Hill
Hamden, CT 06519
Magazine Article Index

Aeromodeller
Argus Hse, Boundary Way
Hemel Hempstead Herts
HP2 7ST ENGLAND

Flying Models Magazine
PO Box 700
Newton, NJ 07860
(973) 383-3355

Hannan's Runway
PO Box 210
Magalia, CA 95954
(503) 873-6421
Fine Modeling Books

McCombs, William F.
PO Box 763576
Dallas, TX 75224
Books on Model Aero Data

Model Airplane News
251 Danbury Road
Wilton, CT 07897
(203) 834-2900

Zaic Yearbooks
Box 135
Northridge, Ca 91328
Filled With Info & Plans

KITS & MATERIALS

A-J Funpak
Box 548
Oregon City, OR 97045
Catapult Gliders

Aerodyne
1924 E. Edinger
Santa Ana, CA 92705
(714) 258-0805
OT Kits & Electronic Scales

Aerospace Composites
PO Box 16621
Irvine, CA 92714
(510) 352-2022
High Tech Materials

America's Hobby Center
146 W. 22 Street
New York, NY 10011
(212) 675-8922
Large Mail Order Stock

Andercraft CC
PO Box 443
Sanlamhof 7532
Republic of So. Africa

Balsa USA
PO Box 164
Marinette, WI 54143
Balsa

Blue Ridge Models
PO Box 429
Skyland, NC 28776
Fine FF Kits

Brown Jr. Motors
PO Box 77
Pine Grove Mills, PA 16868
CO2 Motors

Campbell's Custom Kits
7233 Signature Lane
San Antonio, TX 78263
(210) 649-3980
FF Kits

Campbell Model Supply
37742 Carson St.
Farmington Hills, MI 48331
Kits, Light Tissue

Composite Structures
PO Box 642
Tehachapi, CA 93581
(800) 338-1278
High Tech Materials

Comet Models
3630 S. Iron St.
Chicago, IL 60609
Scale Kits

Copter Concepts
832 Salem Lane
Carpenterville, IL 60110
Rubber Copter Kits

Cox Hobbies
(see Estes)

Dare Designs
Box 521
Cumberland, MD 21502
(301) 722-0356
Beginner's & OT Kits

Davis Model Products
Box 141
Milford, CT 06460
(203) 877-1670
Diesel Fuel, CO2 conversions, Jetex Motors

Diels Engineering
PO Box 263
Amherst, OH 44001
Rubber Scale Kits

DuBois, Gene
PO Box 30053
Acushnet MA 02743
Rubber Scale Kits

EMPS
PO Box 134
Robesonia, PA 19551
Elec Motors & Supplies

Easy Built Models
PO Box 425
Lockport, NY 14095
FF &RC Kits

Estes
PO Box 227
Penrose, CO 81240
Cox Engines, Rockets

FAI Model Supply
PO Box 366
Sayre, PA 18840
(717) 882-9873
Kits, Tan II Rubber

Paul K. Guillow
40 New Salem St.
Wakefield, MA 02184
Beginner's Build-by-Number
Kits, Fine Scale Kits
(617) 245-5255

Herr Engineering Co.
1431 Chaffee Dr, Ste 3
Titusville, FL 32780
(407) 264-2488
Fine Scale Kits

Hobby Hideaway
RR2 Box 19
Delavan, IL 61734
Kits, Diesels

Hobby Supply South
1720 Mars Hill Rd, Ste 8365
Acworth, GA 30101
(770) 974-0843

Indoor Model Supply
1887 West Haven
NW Salem, OR 97304
(503) 370-6350
Indoor Supplies & Kits

Jones, Jim
36631 Ledgestone
Mt. Clemens, MI 48043
Balsa & Rubber Strippers

Micro Air
PO Box 1129
Richland, WA 99352
Simple Gram Scale

Micro-X
PO Box 1063
Lorain, OH 44055
(216) 282-8354
Indoor Kits & Supplies

Mid-West Products
Education Prods. Div.
400 So. Indiana St.
Hobart, IN 46342
(800) 348-3497
School class packs designed for
national competition

Model Research Labs
25108 Marguerite #160
Mission Viejo, CA 92692
High Tech Materials

Nowlen Aero
139 Boardwalk
Greenbrae, CA 94904
Peanut Kits

Peck Polymers
PO Box 710399
Santee, CA 92072
(619) 448-1818

Penn Valley Hobby Center
837 W. Main St.
Lansdale, PA 19446
(215) 855-1268
Many FF Kits & Supplies

RN (see Aerodyne)

Scale Flight Model Co.
Old Fashioned Rubber Powered
Model Airplane Kits, Authentic
Reproductions from the 1930's
and '40's! (See Penn Valley
Hobby Center)

SIG Mfg.
401 S. Front St.
Montezuma, IA 50171
(515) 623-5154
Modeler's Supermarket

ScienText, Inc
48 Whitney St.
Westport, CT 06880
Fine Scale Kits

Superior Props
60375 W. Spruce
LaCombe, LA 70445

VL Products
7871 Alabama Ave. #16
Canoga Pk, CA 91304
Elec Motors

Walston, Jim
725 Cooper Lake Rd SE
Smyrna, GA 30080
Lost Model Locator

PLANS & INFO

Aero Era
5955 SW Glenbrook Rd
Beaverton, OR 97005
Peanut & Grpnut Scale

Aero Plans
8931 Kittyhawk Ave.
Los Angeles, Ca 90045
Plans & Plan Books

Airdevil Model Co.
4304 Madison Ave.
Trumbull, Ct 06611
Flying Aces Plans

Bell Model Aircraft Co
650 Pine Crest Drive
Largo, FL 34640
(813) 584-4003
Scale Kits & Plans

Ben Buckle
9 Islay Crescent
Highworth, Witts
SN6 7HL UK (Many OT Plans)
Many OT Plans

Clements, Vern
308 Palo Alto
Caldwell, ID 83605
Many OT Plans

Cottage Wings
1310 Monache Ave
Porterville, CA 93257
Source Listing

Cleveland Models
PO Box 55962
Indianapolis, IN 46205
(317) 681-1444
Fine Scale Model Plans

Flying Aces Models
1564A Fitzgerald Dr
Pinole, CA 94564
No Cal Plans

Gleason Enterprises
705-10 Ave NW
Ausitn, MN 55912
Vast Plan Catalogue

Hunt, Allen
Box 726
Dunbar, WV 25064
Large OT Plan List

Lidberg, Al
1008 Baseline Rd.
Suite 1074
Tempe, AZ 85283
OT Kits Reduced Size

Midkiff, Mike
420 Lake Shore Dr.
Hot Springs, AR 71913
FAC Scale Plans

Northrup, Bill
2019 Doral Ct
Henderson, NV 89014
OT MB Mag Plans

Pond, John
PO Box 90310
San Jose, CA 95109
Most OT Plans

Scale Model Research
3114 Yukon
Costa Mesa, CA 92626
Scale Info

Thompson, Bruce
328 St Germain Ave
Toronto, Ont CANADA
M5M 1W3
Plans From Old Mags